LB1028.5 .S233 1999
013
Salt
196
Hit
pro

2003 02 18

Other Beeline Books Include:

The Publishing Center
How to Create a Successful Publishing Center in Your School, Church, or Community Group

The Treasured Mailbox
How to Use Authentic Correspondence with Children, K–6

Inside the Classroom
Teaching Kindergarten and First Grade

Write-A-Thon
How to Conduct a Writing Marathon in Your Third- to Fifth-Grade Class

The Magical Classroom
Exploring Science, Language, and Perception with Children

Walk This Way!
Classroom Hikes to Learning

Kids on the 'Net
Conducting Internet Research in K–5 Classrooms

The Young Author Festival Handbook
What Every Planner Needs to Know

Look—and Learn!
Using Picture Books with Children Grades Five and Up

Writing Rules!
Teaching Kids to Write for Life, Grades 4–8

Hit Enter
50+ Computer Projects for K–5 Classrooms

Elin Kordahl Saltveit

Heinemann
Portsmouth, NH

*To my husband, Mark (the writer in our family),
for believing I had good ideas,
encouraging me to write a book,
and making life so exciting.
I put down the ideas
but you made them readable.*

Heinemann
A division of Reed Elsevier Inc.
361 Hanover Street
Portsmouth, NH 03801–3912
http://www.heinemann.com

Offices and agents throughout the world

© 1999 by Elin Kordahl Saltveit

All rights reserved. No part of this book may be reproduced in any form or by any electronic or mechanical means, including information storage and retrieval systems, without permission in writing from the publisher, except by a reviewer, who may quote brief passages in a review. Projects may be photocopied for classroom use only.

The author and publisher wish to thank those who have generously given permission to reprint borrowed material:

Figures 5–2, 5–3, 6–1, and 10–1 © 1999 The Learning Company, Inc. Screen shots provided by KidPix Studio v.1.01.

Figure 5–4 screen shot reprinted by permission from Microsoft Corporation.

Library of Congress Cataloging-in-Publication Data
Saltveit, Elin Kordahl, 1964–
 Hit enter : 50+ computer projects for K–5 classrooms /
 Elin Kordahl Saltveit.
   p.   cm.
 "Beeline books."
 ISBN 0-325-00081-6
  1. Education, Elementary—Computer-assisted instruction.
  2. Computers—Study and teaching (Elementary). I. Title.
 LB1028.5.S233   1999
 372.133'4—dc21   99-10533
                                                     CIP

Editor: Amy L. Cohn
Production: Elizabeth Valway
Interior design: Greta D. Sibley & Associates
Cover design: Darci Mehall, Aureo Design
Manufacturing: Louise Richardson

Printed in the United States of America on acid-free paper
03 02 01   VP   2 3 4 5

Contents

Acknowledgments viii

Introduction ix

Chapter 1 How I Learned (Through Mistakes) 1

Chapter 2 How You Can Learn (Besides Reading This Book) 6

Chapter 3 Guidelines for Getting Started 11

Chapter 4 Start Small, Start Simple 17

    Editing and Autobiographies 19
    Dictate a Story 19
    Easy-to-Make Books 20
    Copying and Pasting Text Programs 21
    Summarize in Twenty Words or Less 21
    Simple Alphabet or Number Books 22
    Alliterative Alphabet Book 23
    Food Can Labels and Ingredients 24
    Commemorative Postage Stamps 24
    Cryptic Treasure Maps 25
    Floor Plans 26
    Addition and Subtraction Pictures 26

        Representations of 6   27
        Alliterative Math Sentences   27
        Fractions   27
        Labeling Insects   27
        Animal Habitats   29
        Letter Sounds   30
        Acrostic Poetry   31

Chapter 5   *Remember Which Comes First—The Computer or Your Curriculum*   32
        Math Problems and Coins   33
        Pie Recipes   34
        Venn Diagrams   36
        Patterns   39
        Digital Cameras and Math Activities   40
        Pen Pal Letters   41
        Shape Ideas   41
        Current Events and Class Newspapers   42
        Primary Source Materials, Clip Art, and Colonial America   43
        Digital Portfolios   44
        A Typical School Day Web Page   44
        The Year-in-Review Web Site   45
        Multiple "Zoos" and Grouping   46
        Books of 100   47
        Food Groups   48
        Collective Nouns   48
        Animated Life Cycles   49

Chapter 6   *Learn from Your Students*   50
        Navajo Rugs and Symmetry   51
        Maps and Stamps   52

Chapter 7   *Accept a Little Chaos*   54

Chapter 8   *Team Up Your Students*   56
        Peer Editing and E-mail   57

	Electric Songs 57
	Truck Stacks 58
	City Guide 59
Chapter 9	*Have Fun* 60
	Digital Field Trip 60
	Altered Images 61
	Analogies and Scanning Hands 62
	Clip Art Leaves 62
	Make Animated and Noisy Spanish Cartoons 63
	Planet Day 64
Chapter 10	*Avoid Hardware- and Software-Specific Projects* 65
	Web Scavenger Hunt 66
	Create Graphs from Scratch 67
	Make a Misleading Graph 69
Chapter 11	*Make Sure Students Do the Work, Not You* 70
	Templates: You Start It, the Kids Finish It 71
	Pack Your Suitcase! 73
Chapter 12	*Decide If the Computer Is the Right Tool* 74
Chapter 13	*What Next?* 81
Appendix	*Basic Preparation Rules* 84

Acknowledgments

Thanks to the teachers that taught me—my elementary schools in Kuwait, Libya, Nigeria, the United Kingdom, the United States, and Saudi Arabia, and my teachers and colleagues at West High School, U.C. Berkeley, the Timilty Middle School, Lesley College, Sleepy Hollow Elementary, the Schools of the Sacred Heart, and the University of San Francisco. To my amazing colleagues at the Schools of the Sacred Heart for generously sharing ideas and always trying something new, and to the administration for their enormous support and encouragement over the years. Thanks especially to my fellow teachers Jeff Cohen, Chuck McAfee, Mary Rerisi-Patota, Tre Frane, Janet Graeber, Carol Sauer, Lori Saltveit, Jamie Sullivan, Marilyn Schaumburg, Caroline Cinti, Hoover Chan, Tracy Sena, Jason Hovey, Chris Corrigan, and Joanne Oppenheimer for putting up with me and teaching me so much. To my terrific students over the years who always took my ideas to higher levels. To Eileen Kordahl (my mom), Taryn Laraja, Susan Reid, Ted Saltveit, Carol Sauer, and Alexa Stuart for your excellent educational critiques of my manuscript. Much love to my parents for your limitless enthusiasm for, support for, and interest in whatever I do, and more concretely, for babysitting Anna, time after time, so I could write. To Anna Banana for being such a good baby. Finally, thanks to John Wright for getting me this gig and Amy L. Cohn (and the crew at Heinemann) for helping me craft the result.

Introduction

I never planned to write books about computers in education, but computers have been in schools for more than fifteen years and teachers still struggle with how to use them. I've looked for a good book to guide me and still haven't found one, so here I am.

Even now there aren't any good books about integrating computers into curriculum in a way that will outlive operating systems, software, the Mac/PC debate, and the Internet as we know them. Veteran teachers know that technical details are not as important as educational goals but are left on their own to figure out how computers can actually help them teach.

The important part of teaching with computers is not the computers—it's the teaching. Computers as a tool can help you teach concepts. But this has little to do with the details of hardware, software, or the Internet. Specific computer skills are educationally trivial, and the only thing we know for certain about computers in the future is that they will change dramatically.

Computer education isn't the sum of your hardware; it's what you do with it. No matter how technology changes, a good education will always be based on good teaching and students' abilities to share and access information. Fundamental education—finding new ways to teach and support reading, writing, math, and science—uses the general advantages that all computers share (editing, manipulating graphics and data, layout and design, and copying and pasting).

We're just beginning to understand how computers can help you teach the fundamentals, and how they don't. You are the only one who can decide how, and when, to use this tool. If you try some of these projects, you will begin to find unique ways to make technology useful for you and your students. Of course, you will probably end up with some very different projects, ones that work better for you. This book is simply an attempt to start the process.

After thirteen years of making mistakes, weathering many technical problems and generations of computers, I've ironed out many simple, surefire, project-based approaches to get you started. Once you've completed a dozen projects with your students, you'll see limitless ways to use technology. These project ideas will continue to be effective as technology changes. Computers are a tricky tool to integrate, but with proven ways to get started you'll catch on and be able to adapt to changing technology.

You can just photocopy one of these projects half an hour before class and wing it. And it will work fine. But if you can work through the project ahead of time and start to alter it to your needs, you'll see the real value of computers as a tool. By the time you repeat the project next year, you'll probably have made it your own.

Chapter 1

How I Learned (Through Mistakes)

It took me a long time to work out the projects in this book. Now I can see why; I was learning to teach at the same time I was learning about integrating computers into my classroom. Once I became a better teacher, the same successful principles directed my work with computers. Hopefully, I can save you some of the hard work (and late nights) that punctuated my journey.

 **School**

When I was at U.C. Berkeley finishing my math degree, a professor told me I could do bigger things than "just be a teacher." He meant to encourage me, but I had no desire to be an actuary, an engineer, a programmer, a mathematician, or a statistician. A fellow math student was going into teaching, and my mom had been an excellent teacher for decades. I decided to follow their leads and become a high school math teacher.

My credential program (1986) taught me nothing about educational technology (other than how to run a slide projector and thread a movie). I moved to Boston and landed a job as a remedial math teacher in the inner-city Roxbury neighborhood.

As a perky new teacher in the Boston Public Schools, I immediately noticed an abandoned but surprisingly well-equipped computer lab down the hall from my classroom. I had written BASIC and PASCAL computer programs to run algorithms. How much harder could it be to use computers with fourteen-year-olds?

I took my students to the lab and used the software I found—BASIC and some Sunburst programs (*The Pond, Safari Search*). The kids enjoyed using computers, and the software reinforced critical thinking skills. Most important, going to the computer lab got us out of my windowless, seventy-square-foot classroom.

My understanding of how to teach with computers was very limited. I'm embarrassed to remember a conflict I had with a language arts teacher on campus. She wanted to do word-processing projects with her students and I thought that was a frivolous use of computer time. Back then, I thought computers should only be used in highly technical problem-solving ways. Ouch!

After helping myself to the lab for some time, I was stopped in the teachers' room by a tall, intimidating teacher responsible for the lab's maintenance. "You can't just go in and use the lab. What credentials do you have for teaching computers?" he barked.

I replied, "What credentials do *you* have?"

"A master's degree in computer education from Lesley College," he sneered.

Mostly out of stubbornness, I announced right there that I would get one, too. I enrolled in the program (and finished my degree at the University of San Francisco). To be honest, I thought this would just be some dumb program with nothing I could *really* learn. I signed up just to spite him. Instead, it began my journey toward real understanding of how to integrate computers *into* curriculum. The courses prompted me to change how I teach and helped me look creatively at how to improve student learning with technology.

These programs taught me a lot in an accelerated way—things that would have taken me years to learn on my own—because there were no books like this one to help me get started. All of the available books were software-specific or how-to programming books. None showed general methods for integrating computers into my teaching.

A big focus of the program at Lesley College (back in the mid-1980s) was Logo. This program lets kids command a small virtual "turtle" to move forward, back, right, and left, and to draw pictures, among other things. Sitting in my graduate classes, I thought this software was the greatest thing around. I could see applications for grades K–12. It made the kids think and reinforced concepts of length, angles, and polygons.

But back in the real world, I found that Logo took me a lot of time to prepare, and even more time for my students to learn (especially those in the K–3 grades). Usually the software drove my lesson plans instead of the other way around. It wasn't simple or easy to implement.

Luckily, the rest of the classes in the program focused on general principles: software evaluation, software design, and multimedia techniques. We were constantly reviewing software and discussing potential uses together.

Failures

Back at my school, I now had starting points to try with my students. I made a lot of mistakes. Fortunately, I didn't give up, and I wrote the agony off as part and parcel of those early years that teachers endure as they learn how to teach. Looking back, I'm not sure whether my mistakes had more to do with computers or my effort to become an effective teacher.

Increasingly, though, I saw the magic of computers. They made concepts easier and quicker to teach, and kids who were normally difficult or uninterested in "boring" subjects would suddenly focus when using the computer. This was a way to reach kids who had different learning styles. I found that they all met with success, not just the kids who usually did well.

My big pitfall early on was thinking that every project should be hard and complicated, the way I saw computers in the 1980s. My projects were lumbering behemoths, elaborate and time-consuming.

After three years of teaching math in Boston, I returned to California and took a job as academic computer coordinator for the Schools of the Sacred Heart in San Francisco. Now I had to teach parents and teachers, as well as students, how to use computers.

I was trained to teach math to sixth through twelfth graders, but now my classes included kindergartners through high school seniors. My hands got clammy when the kindergartners showed up—they were so young! Sometimes they'd hold the mouse like a TV remote control, pointing in the air at the computer screen. Within a few weeks, though, I got over my fears. The help of the K–5 classroom teachers who came to the lab with their students was invaluable. Without their expertise and intimate knowledge of how their students learned best, I'd have been lost. I continue to learn from them.

After my first year, I began to present what I thought were snazzy ideas at conferences. The first was one I co-designed with Lori Martinez, now my sister-in-law. Our students created an electronic story with pictures, sound, animations, and digitized video. In 1991, this was no easy task, but we had an excellent, well-funded computer lab (and still do).

We worked our tails off and were very proud. The final product was pretty neat, but the teachers ended up doing most of the work instead of the students. I thought this project was "where-it-was-at" and would surely make an impression.

Instead, the more seasoned participants at my workshop barely blinked. How could they begin to think about doing a similar project with marginal equipment and little time? What exactly had the students learned? Was the product overwhelming the process?

 Successes

Embarrassed by this flop, I began to think "simple and elegant." My time was limited, too. Couldn't I construct small and manageable projects that would use the computer to teach difficult concepts so teachers would be more willing to try them? If the kids could create the projects from start to finish, it would save time for both the classroom teacher and me, and teach the kids computer skills while reinforcing their classroom lesson.

When I began presenting easy-to-integrate ideas at conferences with Marilyn Schaumburg (a creative computer teacher at my school), we were very nervous. We'd decided to share twenty-five ideas in forty minutes, bang

bang bang, because that was the kind of presentation we wanted to attend. But we didn't know if we were on the right track with our general approach —simple computer projects packed with learning. All of the other conference presenters were sharing lofty project ideas that required cutting-edge technology and lots of time.

Fortunately, teachers at conferences received our ideas warmly, even hotly. Crowds grew until there were two hundred or more; they even sat quietly and took notes (unlike other sessions where folks left early and noisily). And they started asking if I had a book they could buy.

Chapter 2
How You Can Learn (Besides Reading This Book)

This chapter discusses some ways to learn new ideas and keep up to date after you start teaching. In the end, you need to decide what will work for you and your students; your classroom experience will be your best guide.

Study other people's project ideas—including mine—with a critical eye. Some projects may have suggested grade levels or software. You might have to adapt to the grade level of your students. Computer resources also vary; you have to decide if the project is doable with your equipment. The best ideas don't usually require much equipment.

 Attend Conferences

Conferences are the easiest way to learn new ideas and stay abreast of changes. These don't need to be expensive national conventions in other cities; local ones are often among the best.

Your time is precious. It's hard to get away from the classroom, because the preparation time for being away is almost as much as for staying to teach the class! So make the most of a conference. Attend as many presentations as you can and get handouts right away; if you've picked a loser session, leave and go to another.

I present at many conferences, and I'm one of the worst-behaved conference attendees. If I'm sitting in a session that isn't what I expected, or if presenters read from their handouts, or the equipment isn't working, I leave.

If no other session interests you, wander the exhibit floor and grill the (often bored!) exhibitors. They are a captive audience and welcome your questions. Play with their computers and software. Or talk to other session dropouts who are hanging out in hallways waiting for the next session to begin.

It's hard to get away, but a good conference is a wonderful way to gain perspective, build camaraderie, and acquire inspiration. At the very least, plan to leave with a few new ideas you will start using. Have simple goals—once you return, the nuts and bolts of daily school life will again swamp you.

 Present at Conferences

After you've developed some ideas you like, start sharing them. Submit proposals to present at conferences. I've learned so much from folks who attend my presentations. They'll e-mail, write, or share ideas right after a session.

Don't worry if you're not a "techie." There will always be folks who can fix computers one-handed in the dark, but it takes much more to figure out creative, educational uses of computers that help your students learn better. You'll probably run into some humorless techies who need to show off by asking difficult technical questions, but don't let them bother you. Everyone else sees through them, too. Just gently steer the conversation back to education and move on.

 Brainstorm with Colleagues

It can be hard to find the time, but spend fifteen minutes bouncing ideas off of someone else at your school. If you have computer resource personnel, make sure to seek them out and put them to work. They'll be thrilled that you approached them. If you don't have such personnel, try your librarian (librarians are great for guiding students' research and planning projects) or find out who is good with computers and willing to share ideas.

Don't be afraid to ask for help. Too often we're isolated in our classrooms. But who doesn't like to be asked for advice? Most teachers will give more than you request. It makes folks feel good, saves your time, and generates terrific ideas for your students.

If you are the computer resource person, be sure to work with classroom teachers. They know their curriculums and students intimately. All of our projects are collaborations between classroom and computer teachers.

I love the "ping-pong" effect of brainstorming. I usually ask what areas teachers will be covering with their students. They mention some things, I toss out a few possibilities, and we end up coming up with great ideas for the class. This way, too, everyone has ownership. (I know this is a smarmy term, but it describes an important reality.)

After you've developed a useful idea, share it! Computer ideas don't belong to any one person. If we're all developing computer projects tied to the curriculum, strangers will develop similar ideas. We're using the same machines to teach the same things, after all.

I remember when a colleague, Tracy Sena, came to visit my school years ago. As I began to show her our projects, she would occasionally exclaim, "I do something like that! I have kids create pie graphs by drawing circles and estimating parts, too." Without ever having met or spoken, we thought alike. She felt validated because, working in isolation, she had come up with the same effective approaches we had. And of course, we felt validated, too.

You *could* come up with a brilliant way to teach that no one has ever thought of before, but you're much more likely to improve a good thing someone else is doing, or to have your ideas improved by them. So don't worry about hiding and protecting your ideas. Share them and develop them.

Take Risks and Try New Ideas

Your first try with a new idea may result in anything from disaster to unexpected success, or both. That's the way things work. Try the idea and see how you could improve it next time—saving yourself time, making it simpler, getting students to do more of the work, or packing more learning into the lesson. Know that you'll have to work out kinks and improve on the idea the second time around. Kids even like to hear that they are the first to try something as a test group.

Rarely, but sometimes, an idea has no redeeming value and should be dropped from your repertoire of ideas. That's okay, too. Don't despair.

 ## Go Back to School

Although continuing one's education is good for all of us, a master's degree can be expensive and hard to schedule. It is not the only way to learn what you need to know, but it can definitely be worthwhile. I completed my master's degree at two places, Lesley College and the University of San Francisco. The first institution emphasized current technology in schools, software evaluation, and practical, doable integration. The second had a more philosophical approach and encouraged us to look at cutting-edge technology and how we might implement it in our classrooms. The two were perfect complements. I got caught up with what was current and then had a chance to explore what was coming in the near future. The minute I completed my degree, I was on my own again—armed with new knowledge but needing to keep up to date.

 ## Read Computer-Related Articles

Although keeping up with professional magazines can be nearly impossible once school whips into its usual frenzy, pick up random (often free) subscriptions to computer-related magazines and browse them when possible. There's usually one good article or nugget of information per magazine. Go to a conference and get some free samples and subscriptions. Ask colleagues to share interesting articles with you. Forward articles and magazines to your administrators to keep them current. Recommend articles for parents to read.

Try to read more than just educational magazines. Most newspapers now have computer and technology sections, and much of the business section involves some aspect of technology. Sometimes I even scan computer mail-order catalogs, which involve little reading at all, just to see what's new.

Go On-Line

More teachers and groups are posting computer ideas on the Internet. You can read articles on-line, post help questions, or join a Listserv for e-mailed information. Visit my Web site for current sites to visit and Listservs to join (http://www.realchange.org/compideas).

Chapter 3
Guidelines for Getting Started

I'm not a big one for rules. "Do what works" is usually my motto. But some approaches simply work better with computer projects and kids, time after time. I try to keep these in mind each time I plan a project.

Here is a quick list of the guidelines I follow. There are a few more basic guidelines in the Appendix on page 84. In the rest of the book, I'll discuss each one the way I might if I met you during a workshop, at a conference, or on a plane trip—with examples, war stories, and digressions.

 Start Small, Start Simple

I made the mistake early on of thinking that a computer project must be immense and flashy to really count. Kids would only be interested in doing something spectacular, and computers would only be recognized as a useful tool if they did something very complicated. I think I got this idea from journals, professional magazines, and conferences where folks were always showing off their masterpieces.

I was wrong. Those epic projects took too much of my time, and I ended up doing most of the work behind the scenes. These projects didn't excite students; they bored them because they weren't involved enough.

There is no need for that, especially if you are just getting started. If kids have room to be creative, they don't need clever project designs to be engaged. They should put their energy into the project's concepts, not advanced computer commands.

Start with a small, simple project that supports something your students are already learning. There are two opposite approaches to developing a new idea:

1. Begin with content you are very familiar with. This way you know the subject well and only have to focus on a new technical tool.

2. Choose a content area you've never really liked. A new approach will help keep your interest, and you (and your students) have little to lose by trying something new.

Whichever approach you take, keep the computer skills simple and give students free rein to demonstrate the concepts of your main subject, whether it's writing, science, or math.

Remember Which Comes First— The Computer or Your Curriculum

Unlike the old chicken-egg conundrum, we know the answer to this one. Unfortunately, some technology-dazzled teachers forget this. Make sure you're doing things with technology that support, enrich, enhance, or extend an idea. Don't indulge the temptation to pursue interesting technical challenges for their own sake.

I think many folks are reluctant to start teaching with computers because they think it's just more work, in addition to the existing curriculum. Actually, a good computer project helps you teach your existing subjects more quickly and thoroughly. Students will pick up the computer skills they need no matter what your project is, so focus on teaching content.

Learn from Your Students

I was watching a new teacher start the year by demonstrating a drawing program to first graders, and she was in trouble. She tried to draw with the pen tool, but nothing appeared no matter how much she clicked around because the pen color was set to white. I considered stepping in, but before I could one of the kids said, "Try picking a different color?"

Even the littlest kids can be helpful. Give them a chance to teach you. Computers are the first place I have seen where the collaborative, coaching model of teaching actually works in real life. Kids and teachers really can learn together instead of perpetuating the usual scenario in which teachers are the sole source of information.

There was a time when you could know it all in computers. There weren't many software titles, the Internet had limited resources, and machines couldn't do as much. Now, there is far too much material to even try to master it all. The only way to stay on top is to listen to other people, listen to your students, ask lots of questions, and read when you can, either in print or on-line. You will then model for students the only way that they will be able to keep up with rapidly changing technology through their lifetimes.

 ## Accept a Little Chaos

It's critical to have a well-thought-out plan when you start a project—winging it just won't work. See Appendix A, Basic Preparation Rules. Once you start, though, be ready for a 180-degree change if the technology goes wrong or a student has a bright idea. Never feel you need to know it all, or that you MUST stick to your original plan. Once a good project gets going, kids will talk and compare notes, computers will crash, someone will suggest something completely different than what you thought—and that's all on a *good* day.

Don't try to eliminate this spontaneity. Not only will you fail and drive yourself crazy trying, but you will also miss some of the real magic that creative, open-ended computer projects make possible.

Team Up Your Students

Kids like to work together, and they often end up answering each other's technical questions more quickly than you ever could. Pair kids when they are trying a challenging new computer skill or doing an involved project that has many steps.

It's even more fun to create one big project from everyone's contributions. For example, combine individual computer drawings into a class book or slideshow. Some programs, like *Hyperstudio*, *KidPix*, *Slideshow*, and Microsoft *PowerPoint*, let you gather projects together into a continuously running show. Seeing everyone else's work reinforces the teaching concept over and over while encouraging collaboration.

I love watching kids present animations they create, such as computer drawings of seeds growing into flowers (see Animated Life Cycles in Chapter 5). The class watches all of the drawings combined together: seeds to roots to stems to leaves to flowers, over and over, each piece drawn differently and imaginatively. This is wonderful reinforcement.

Have Fun

You don't need to convince kids to use computers. They love them. Just make sure you have fun, too.

Dream up projects where kids will be looking at each other's computers, talking, working, and even giggling. Computer projects don't have to be serious. Using a computer by yourself is impersonal, so make sure that kids interact when they use them. When used collaboratively, computers don't isolate individuals; they help develop relationships and new perspectives on learning. And they're a lot more fun.

Avoid Hardware- and Software-Specific Projects

In 1965, Intel executive Gordon Moore predicted that computer chips would double in power every eighteen months (Moore's Law), and this has been amazingly accurate ever since. The result, of course, is that computers and software change dramatically every year. No one knows what Internet browsers or operating systems will look like in a few years. Web sites change even faster—every few months or even daily.

The only way to handle this is to keep your projects skill-specific, not software-specific. Design them for general functions of software (drawing, word processing) rather than for specific programs and their advanced, unique commands (no matter how impressive). This way, when technology changes, you will be able to adapt your projects easily without losing sight of the educational objectives.

 ## Make Sure Students Do the Work, Not You

Make sure your students do as much of the work as possible. Students learn by doing. If they are half as impatient as I am, they'd rather be working on the project than listening to you. Avoid setting up ready-made files on every computer. Isn't there a way the kids can begin to do this themselves? Slowly build their skills so they can. Start by having them at least open the ready-made files you've created. Move them to opening programs and creating new documents. Then show them how to make their own projects from start to finish. They'll be more involved, and you'll have more time to answer questions or help them learn the core subject. This will save you time, too.

When your projects are too complicated or flashy, you inevitably end up doing too much of the work, either in complicated preparations, or—worse yet—as you run around the classroom finishing tasks for befuddled students. You're also setting yourself up for technical problems. The more complicated your setup, the more can go wrong.

 ## Decide If the Computer Is the Right Tool

Is the computer the right tool for *all* students *all* the time? Of course not. It certainly supports a variety of learning styles. A computer can be the most patient tutor ever and make someone's work look as good as the effort that went into it. It will help with spelling again and again, provide a forum for different ideas (e-mail, bulletin boards, Listservs, Web pages), and give access to most information in which a student is interested. But it's not the only tool and shouldn't be used for everything.

Can the project be photocopied instead of scanned? Would the illustrations look nicer if drawn by hand and colored with markers, crayons, or pencils? Will the audience listen better if the child is talking live rather than recording sounds to disk? Would it be easier to make a phone call than search the Web? Would the information be easier to receive via fax? Or would it be easier to just ask a teacher, parent, or librarian a question than go on-line?

Don't make problems and extra work for yourself. If it's easier to do a project WITHOUT the computer, don't use it. But if the computer helps present information in a clearer and more interesting way, makes large piles of information manageable, or supports instruction about a concept, use it.

The computer shouldn't be the point of a lesson. It's not a subject; it's just a tool you use to make a concept as clear as possible. Because it's your most expensive tool, there's a tendency to use it for everything to justify the expense. The only thing you need to justify as an educator is how well your students learn.

Chapter 4
Start Small, Start Simple

Simple goals, simple concepts, simple approaches.

I mean *really* simple, especially if you are going to be learning computer skills along with your students. With young kids, don't forget they're often getting used to the mouse, keyboard, and operating system, to opening and closing folders and applications, and so forth; if they only write a few sentences for a project, they've taken many other steps to get to that point. In the upper grades, many students already know the basic computer skills (cutting and pasting, for example), but they will still need some tips from teachers on the easiest ways to do things. Here are some tips to keep things simple:

- Have at least one good reason for turning to computers to teach an idea, even with the simplest projects.

- Keep the project open-ended! In other words, assign a goal (not a series of specific tasks). Keep the rules and structure you impose to a minimum. If you let students embellish the basic concept, you encourage creativity without creating any additional work for yourself. You also minimize the chance of computer problems.

- Stick with open-ended tools (like standard drawing or word-processing programs) instead of lots of specialized software titles.

If I were to start all over again, I'm confident that I could teach grades K–12 all year with a word processor that has basic drawing tools. Most computers come loaded with a free word processor and drawing program. Individual games, simulation tools, and drill-and-practice software have their places, but if resources are limited or you are getting started, use the tools that are already available.

The trick is finding multiple ways to use open-ended tools that have limitless possibilities. By using them, students will learn skills that will last forever.

Have Students Write First Drafts on the Computer

Many teachers have students draft reports with pen and paper first. After the teacher has corrected their papers, students rewrite on paper, and then enter their work into a word processor, format it, and print. This exercise requires time-consuming retyping into the computer and sends the message that revising your writing is boring and tedious.

Multiple revisions are the key to good writing, and computers make them much easier. Ideas can be copied, cut, and pasted later.

Have kids compose their first draft on the computer (as early as first grade). Students will feel less restricted in getting their ideas down if they know this is really a draft. They can make as many drafts as time and computer access allow. This approach focuses students on improving their writing, not on the frustrating mechanics of producing new drafts by hand.

Even if your students aren't fast keyboarders, the digital editing process is better in the long run. Fellow students can read the information on the screen or via e-mail. Students are more likely to print out copies, distribute them, get some feedback on paper, and incorporate suggestions back on their computer file.

Encourage proper keyboarding techniques as early as third grade (sit up straight, place fingers on the home keys, and so on) every time children input text. Keyboarding is a necessary evil and the focus of a big philosophical debate. However you feel about it, and whatever your own ability level, at least direct your students to push past the hunt-and-peck system.

Project: Editing and Autobiographies

Even first graders can begin to edit. Toward the end of the year, we took a digital picture of each student and pasted it into a separate word processor file. Students opened their files, looked at their pictures, and wrote about themselves. They composed sentences while sitting at the computer and didn't get a lot done, but we still printed the one, two, or three sentences each of them wrote. During the next week, with their teacher's help, they edited their work. They returned to their file, made corrections, and added a little more. We printed the final autobiographies and put them together into a class book.

Project: Dictate a Story

The youngest students can't type much, but I count their dictation as composing. Here's why.

On the computer, we had kindergarten and first-grade students tell stories. They drew a picture on the computer first, and then looked at it while they explained what was going on. As a middle school teacher new to kindergarten students, I never realized they were creating stories each time they drew.

We had older students type as the kindergartners dictated (parents and aides also work well for this task). Later on, the authors retold their stories, read them, or had the stories reread to them. You may wonder what this has to do with having students compose their writing on the computer. Well, kids *are* composing on the computer. You are modeling what they will do when they begin to write themselves.

I love doing this with kids. Some kids don't have long stories to tell, and you might find yourself prompting them a little ("Why is this dragon flying over the bridge?"). More often you start to worry, as you type and type, that their creative stories might never end! Someday, voice recognition software will alleviate the time spent transcribing or recording, but I'm not sure I'd replace the human connection of kindergartners telling their stories to an adult or older student.

This project would be neat to do via the phone with a remote pen pal (foreign language learners, grandparents, and so on). The kindergartners would call from a school phone and someone at the other end would type up the story. They could then e-mail, fax, or mail the story back to you.

Project: Easy-to-Make Books

Students love making books individually or together with their class. Start their publishing careers early. If you're worried about wasting paper, print on scrap paper. When kids get started writing books, it's hard to stop them. The school secretary and computer labs are a great source of white paper used only on a single side and still in good condition. If you have a recycling team on campus, they can set up some reuse boxes to collect scrap paper, too.

Open your word processor to a new file. Preset the font and size so that it's appropriate for the grade level (increase the size for very young kids so only a few words fill up a page). You could prepare a list of key words (colors, animals, numbers, etc.) for them.

If you have only one computer, rotate students through the station. Otherwise, have a word processor open and ready on all screens (one per student). There are too many steps involved for young children to find, open, and set the font every time they want to write. And writing is really the goal here. It can take a very long time for them to write a few words or even a sentence. I am still learning to give this process plenty of time.

Direct the youngest kids (kindergartners or first graders) to write one sentence per page. You could have a sentence starter, such as "I see (number) (color) (animal)." Show them how to press the enter (or return) key a few times. Then, have them type their names so they can find their own page from the stack that comes out of the printer.

After they write one sentence, print the page. The children should then delete the words they typed and start another sentence or relinquish the computer (if there's only one) so someone else can write. Of course, if a few students have technical problems (it happens) or just a tough day, I might lean over and help them finish their sentences.

After they are done, have them illustrate their page(s) by hand, either in class or in a lab setting. Keep some crayons in the computer lab. It seems odd, but why not? It's a great way to keep everyone engaged in the project, and gives the slower writers or big thinkers time to finish.

Collect all of the pages and staple them together with a blank page on top for the title. You can either make individual books or put them into one class book, depending on your resources.

One creative teacher even brought her "reading" chair (a pint-sized rocking chair) to the lab. When her students were done making a book (usually one with at least five pages), they could read to her or to other students who had finished. It makes a computer lab feel much more like a classroom—which it really is.

With one simple project, children have gained some familiarity with the keyboard, used the delete and enter (or return) keys, practiced putting spaces between words, made sentences, placed periods at the ends of sentences, and practiced vocabulary learned in class.

Project: Copying and Pasting Text Programs

Just recently, after a dozen-plus years of teaching with computers, I had a startling revelation. I realized that my fourth and fifth graders had no idea they could copy and paste text from one program (a word processor) to another (desktop publishing).

They had composed, edited, and fine-tuned paragraphs about colonial history on a word processor. We were pasting up a one-page, two-column newspaper using their text and some pictures. After about ten minutes of watching them type, I realized they were retyping their paragraphs from a computer printout into the desktop publishing program. Ack!

After I showed them how to copy and paste their text into another document, they said things like, "Wow!" and "Cool." I couldn't believe that years of showing kids how to copy and paste graphics hadn't transferred to text. Even with the kids who knew computers well, it just hadn't occurred to them.

Computers do incredible things, and even the most savvy students still need someone to guide them.

Project: Summarize in Twenty Words or Less

Kids are always prone to plagiarize from books. I don't think the habit stems from laziness or the inability to write. When I was a kid, I was always so impressed with how succinctly books would say things that I didn't think I could do better.

You can help students fight that urge and get more involved in writing. Ask your students to write short, concise "bullets" of information from text they are reading. Limit the length of each bulleted item to twenty words or less. (Show them how to execute a word count; this is a feature available in most word processors.)

My fifth-grade students participated in a contest to describe the computer of the future. They had to limit their description to fifty words. There was so much they wanted to say! But they caught on to choosing descriptive words that relayed as much information as full, lengthy sentences. Here's an example:

> The coolest computer is a multimedia center. There is a virtual reality schoolhouse where you learn by playing games. There is a cafeteria with edible food that is all non-fat and good tasting. My teacher would be nice and have an unlimited vocabulary to answer all my questions.

Limiting the length of a description forces students to understand and rephrase concepts. And when they write research reports, you've taught them that it's fine to get ideas from books, but they need to put those ideas in their own words.

At the same time, kids can begin citing sources even in the early grades. Carol Sauer, my school's librarian, has developed some guidelines for getting kids started. Visit her Web site for more details at http://www.sacred.sf.ca.us/library_sites/overview.html.

Avoid Time-Consuming Projects

Students can learn a lot in a thirty-minute, "one-shot-wonder" project. These may be ideal if you have limited lab time, few computers, or a class cut short by an unexpected school activity.

Project: Simple Alphabet or Number Books

Not having a strong K–1 background, I thought it was a waste of time when teachers wanted to make picture books for the alphabet or for numbers 1 through 20. Each child would have one page (e.g., number 4). They were to draw the numeral 4, write the word *four*, and then stamp a picture four times below it. (Stamps are predefined pictures that students can easily place in a drawing, like built-in clip art. Some programs, notably *KidPix*, provide these.) The class would then combine their pages into a class book of the first twenty numbers.

Once I saw the children in action, though, it was undeniable that the one-to-one association of numbers to objects is effective. More important, they liked seeing each other's work and would flip through the books, back in class, during their free time.

To make an alphabet book, divide the alphabet up and let each child choose a letter. In a drawing program, the children should then write that letter on the screen, and draw as many pictures as they can think of (or have room for) that begin with the letter. If you have fewer than twenty-six students, the first to finish can tackle the leftovers. Or you can use them to demonstrate the technique to the class.

Although I often refer to clip art (large collections of pictures ranging from apples to zebras that are easily cut and pasted and added to files), I much prefer kids' original drawings. I never allow my students to frivolously use stamps or clip art; otherwise, all of the pictures just look the same. When we use stamps, it's because they allow the kids to explore an idea differently.

Project: Alliterative Alphabet Book

Either let each child select a favorite letter or assign the letters of the alphabet. First, the child makes a list of all of the words he or she can think of that start with the letter. For example, for *S* the list might look something like this:

Sam	silly	see
slippery	sea	slimy
seal	so	swim
seven	super	sick
salty		

At the computer, the student composes sentences using as many of these words as possible. "See silly Sam the slippery seal swim in the salty sea." (I savor such silly sentences!) Then students illustrate what they write. These sentences can also be shaped around a theme: fall words, holiday words, or science topics. Combine the pages into a class alliterative alphabet book.

Project: Food Can Labels and Ingredients

When kids are studying the basic food groups, have them design a label for a can of healthy soup, listing the ingredients. Students should bring an empty can of soup. Inside they place "ingredients" they make with colored paper.

Then they create the soup's label on the computer. Set up a new word-processing file with a large font size. Students list the contents of their healthy soup ("Ingredients: water, tomatoes, potatoes, carrots, leeks, garlic, salt"). As with ingredient labels found on cans of soups, the ingredients should be listed in order of the amount used, with the largest quantities used listed first. Print the information, cut it out, and glue it to the can. Word processing and editing are reinforced and the computer-generated label makes the can look more "real." Students could draw pictures on the label and even add a bar code.

Project: Commemorative Postage Stamps

Figure 4-1 Commemorative Postage Stamp

Kids love to make their own postage stamps. They include a picture and one key phrase about the picture that sums up a subject they are studying. They draw a stamplike border and add the value of the stamp—any amount they want. Kids usually choose stamp values they consider a fortune—like $5.00.

My favorite stamp was drawn on the computer using only the pencil tool and no colors. The pencil tool is common to most programs with any drawing capabilities. Its icon usually looks like a pencil; it draws a freeform line when you click on it and drag the mouse. The stamp depicted the first female doctor, Elizabeth Blackwell, giving an injection to a little girl sitting on a gurney. The needle was huge, and on close inspection, teeny-tiny tears streamed from the girl's eyes. Imagine receiving a letter—or a medical bill—with that image on the envelope!

The stamp was made by a third grader to celebrate Women's History Month. After studying famous women, this child—as well as her classmates—drew a picture of a noteworthy, well-known woman that illustrated why she has earned a place in history.

You could create stamps related to Black History Month, holidays, sports stars, current events, musicians, scientists, or chemical elements (e.g., a picture, phrase, and value for Argon). Or classes could collect actual stamps featuring these themes.

Project: Cryptic Treasure Maps

When kids are learning about direction and the compass rose (the object that orients the map to north, south, east, and west) let them work in teams to make a cryptic treasure map for a school hunt. Warn them that they will switch with another team and follow that team's map, so they should only do unto others a level of sneakiness that they would want done unto them!

In one class, after hiding goodies around the school, teams of kids made treasure maps showing where the goodies were hidden. In pairs, they drew lines representing walls, hallways, windows, and staircases, and they added pictures of chairs, tables, toilets, staircases, and doorways. After they had the map drawn, they added some cryptic clues for finding the treasure, such as "Albert Einstein likes it here" (for the science room), a picture of a musical note (for the music room), "where little ones play" (the kindergartners' room), and "waste area" (the bathroom).

My fifth-grade students worked in pairs and created devious maps. They employed tools I never knew existed. For example, one team flipped their map so you would have to read it in a mirror (some drawing programs have magic mixing tools that distort drawings). Some drew their maps south-north (instead of the usual north-south) to further complicate things. They were completely engaged, talking about scale and where objects and places belonged, and debating about the perfect word play to create their cryptic clues. Because the computer lets you make changes so easily, they were able to try things to see if they had the proper effect without the risk of having to start all over.

Each team was searching for a small bag of chocolate coins. On the day of the hunt, I saw kids all over our campus reading maps and running in short spurts from spot to spot.

Project: Floor Plans

Have your students create a floor plan of the classroom using drawing tools like the straight-line tool, rectangle tool, eraser, and shading tools. Explain that they should imagine they are looking down, with a bird's-eye view from above the classroom. They should try to keep things in perspective and scale. First, they should draw it exactly as it is. Next, have them draw a floor plan of how they would like it to look. Where should the computer be? How should the desks be arranged? Where can the plants be placed?

You could even take a vote for the best classroom design layout and actually reorganize the room (with teacher veto power, of course). Other variations include making floor plans for their bedrooms or designing an ideal playground.

Project: Addition and Subtraction Pictures

Have your students write a math sentence like "4 + 2 = 6" at the top of their screen. Below the 4 they should place four pictures, below the 2 they should place two pictures, below the 6 they should place six pictures.

For subtraction, they should write a problem like "8 – 4 = 4." Below the 8 they should place eight pictures (e.g., eight light bulbs). Using the pencil tool they should cross out four of the items. What remains is the answer to the problem.

Project: Representations of 6

How many ways are there to add two numbers to make the sum 6? Using careful spacing on the screen, kids should write all of the math sentences they can think of that total 6 (1 + 5 = 6; 2 + 4 = 6; 3 + 3 = 6; 6 + 0 = 6). They should illustrate each math sentence with pictures, as in the previous project.

Project: Alliterative Math Sentences

Divide the alphabet among the students. Have each student write a math sentence such as "I found four fancy Frenchmen each frying four fish fingers. How many fish fingers are there?" Students can then illustrate the math sentence and show the solution. You may want to compile their pages for a class book.

Project: Fractions

Have kids write math sentences that include fractions, such as "I have one apple and gave $\frac{1}{4}$ to Jake and another $\frac{1}{4}$ to George. How much do I have left?" The children can color parts or pull them away to show what remains.

It's interesting to see what kids do with shapes that aren't regular or symmetrical. (See: Navajo Rugs and Symmetry in Chapter 6 to explore symmetry.) How, for example, do you cut a pear into equal parts?

The first time I tried this project, the teacher let the kids draw their fraction pictures, had them print their work at the end of the class, and then saved the files to disk. Between sessions she reviewed their pictures with them and talked about unequal parts. Did it seem like everyone would get an equal part of the pear the way it was cut up? If you were dividing a wedge of fudge cake into 4 parts, would you want a piece that was smaller than someone else's? How should you divide the cake so that if you cut and I choose, we get equal parts?

This was a great lesson, and the kids could go back to their files (one of the computer's most powerful abilities), edit their work, and make it right.

Project: Labeling Insects

I hate projects that ask every student to do the same thing. What's interesting about everyone drawing the same prelabeled bug from a photocopied sheet or book? I wonder if this practice makes children think that every problem has already been solved, and that it's just their turn to copy the answer. This approach seems to be all about right and wrong, with no in-between or fun.

Instead, I always try to get them to interpret or add to the drawing. For example, you can download several pictures of insects from the Internet. With current Macintosh Web browsers you can click on a picture, keep the mouse button depressed for a few seconds, and a menu will appear. Select "copy picture," open a drawing program, and paste the picture directly into a file. With Windows machines, right-click with the mouse and the menu will appear. Have kids label the body parts they are studying on each bug. This way they see a variety of actual insects and have to find the same parts on different insects. If time allows, kids can view pictures on Web pages, select one they like, and then redraw the insect from a different angle, in flight, or after being squashed on a windshield. You can let students draw a bug of their choice or even make up an imaginary insect as long as it contains body parts that define insects: thorax, abdomen, head, wings (optional), and antennae.

Keep Projects Open-Ended

Don't detail everything the student should do. A general subject for kids to draw or write about gives them lots of room to be creative while keeping your workload down.

Many of the projects in this book combine writing and drawing. Here are a few tricks to remember:

- Schedule ample time for the project so students have time to complete important details.
- Ask the kids to do all of their writing FIRST; when they are done they can illustrate the writing. Some kids will spend inordinate amounts of time getting the details of an illustration right instead of concentrating on what you really want them to be learning, which is often expressed in words. (Of course, for some kids drawing first is better. It depends on your lesson objectives and students.)
- Remind them to draw pictures that relate to the story.

It never ceases to amaze me that I have to remind kids to draw pictures specific to what they are writing. Many of the boys I teach wouldn't think twice about putting a picture of an admired Humvee car to illustrate their writing, even if the subject they were studying was a snake.

If some kids are having a hard time getting the writing done and they don't finish the computer illustrations, print the piece anyway. They can illustrate their writing by hand later. Doing all the work on the computer is not necessarily the point of a project.

Project: Animal Habitats

Some ideas are easier to communicate with pictures than with words. Natural habitats, where many life forms coexist in synergy with a particular environment, is one of these. The action in a tide pool or the characteristics of a rotting log are much more easily sketched than described.

Because we also value the precision of writing, have your students combine text and drawing. They can write some bulleted information in a word processor and edit, format, and save, using the powers of a word processor to make their writing the best it can be. Then they can describe their habitats (desert, island reef, and so on) with a picture in their favorite draw/paint program. Finally, they can select the picture and copy and paste it back into the file with their writing.

The concept of copying and pasting between programs is a skill that will be useful no matter how hardware and software change. Students need to know that nothing is static, that work created once can be reused elsewhere (if appropriate). Kids also need to understand that there are very few limitations with their work, and they can pull information from any resource they want.

Word processors are making it increasingly easy to draw within a document. Even so, there will be times that students want to draw in a special drawing program (because of the more sophisticated tools), and then copy and paste their art into their word processors to illustrate a story. Start this with kids as early as first grade. You could place pictures in the scrapbook (on a Macintosh) to make it easier for them to execute.

My third graders have created beautiful drawings of habitats. They have the correct animals, insects, and environmental features of the habitat they are studying (e.g., for a reef they included coral, fish, water, seaweed, and rocks). These pictures are a superb demonstration of their knowledge. After I began outlawing the use of clip art and stamps, their drawings immediately took on abstract and deeper qualities.

Sometimes kids will come to school knowing a drawing program (or at least thinking they do). Usually I find that they have only explored the superficial uses of tools. Once I ask them to use particular tools to draw, or I direct them to some of the hidden special features of drawing tools (like holding down the shift or option keys when drawing, or pulling up optional menus), they find new ways to draw, and they begin to incorporate these in future drawings.

One student studying reefs used a drawing tool that created spirals to portray different colored corals. It was magical and so much more effective than any clip art drawn by a stranger would have been.

Project: Letter Sounds

Many drawing programs have stamps. While they are less creative than original drawings, these are good for the littlest kids.

In this project we use stamps to explore the sounds of beginning letters. Kids in kindergarten type their first names on the screen. For example, little Anna would find stamps beginning with the letter or sound *A* (*apple, ax, ant,* and *anvil*) and place those vertically below the letter *A*. Then she'd find stamps beginning with the same letter or sound as *N* (musical *note, nut,* and *nose*), and so on. If students finish early, they can do the same thing for their last names or a favorite word.

Some letters are harder to find than others, such as *O*. If you can't find an opal, ox, or orangutan, leave a space below the letter and color it with an orange crayon later. You might wonder why a student has placed a tomahawk below the letter *A*. Ask the student why he or she chose it. The student might think of it as an ax, or even an antique.

Within one class, you'll probably have a slow student who barely gets one or two pictures per letter for every student who finds five or ten pictures for each letter and finishes their first *and* last names. But both students are engaged and learning. Sometimes it's not a matter of smarts or quickness; some children may get so involved making their own stamps or pictures that they just have to concentrate on that one thing. So what? Let them do it.

For an interesting variation, older kids learning a second language could do this project in that language, or kids in an ESL program can use it to practice their English.

Project: Acrostic Poetry

Acrostic poetry requires students to write a word (such as *Cathy*) vertically. (The Greek poet Nicander started this in 300 B.C.) To the right of the letter *C*, the student writes a phrase starting with the letter *C*. To the right of the letter *A*, the student composes another phrase starting with that letter, and so on. Here's an example:

C onstantly cheery

A lways a good listener

T hinks about others

H as brown hair

Y odels a lot

To make the most of this as a computer exercise, have students illustrate the poems (time allowing) with the computer drawing tools or by hand. Let them experiment with font styles and sizes.

The acrostic poems some third graders made around Halloween were descriptively gory and bloody, with scary pictures. I loved them! Here's an example:

H eadless horsemen

A ngry skeletons

L oud yells

L aughing ghouls

O gres lurching

W itches staring

E vil elves

E yeballs bleeding

N asty newts

Chapter 5

Remember Which Comes First—The Computer or Your Curriculum

The answer, of course, is your curriculum. Make sure that technology is the tail and that the curriculum is wagging it. Don't change your program to use a new technology just because the school spent $50,000 and wants something to show for it. Also, don't worry about making projects splashy to engage students. Even if your students are more familiar with computers than you are, they will be interested, involved, and unconcerned about your mastery of technology as long as the project is tied to the curriculum.

I've taught children of Microsoft software developers, kids who've left in fourth grade to attend university classes (whether or not this is a good idea), and plenty of naturally curious and skilled techie-kids. These students know a lot about computers and the Internet, but you'd never know it. When they use the computer to learn more about classroom subjects, when they use the computer to present their ideas, they NEVER second-guess me about my computer knowledge, even when they know they know more. They focus on presenting the information they are learning, not just demonstrating computer skills.

These knowledgeable kids, of course, are a great resource. When you encounter mysterious viruses or technical problems, don't be too proud to get their help.

Kill Two Birds with One Computer—Teach Two Things at the Same Time

You don't need to teach computer skills per se, because students are picking them up any time they use the computer. So focus on the curriculum side. As long as you explain any unfamiliar computer techniques as you go, they will learn both.

Project: Math Problems and Coins

The first-grade teachers in my school wanted to find ways to use the computer to expand the ways in which their students learned about coins, studied the concepts of amounts, and mastered making change. We started by scanning some coins as clip art to explore the computer function of copy and paste and to address the curriculum need to identify coins.

But what next? I could only think to have the students write problems such as "I need twenty-three cents" and then copy and paste coins to make the amount. I wasn't satisfied with this, however, and began asking my colleagues for help.

One teacher suggested having the students, in pairs, write a "story." Another recommended adding a clip art change purse for "holding" the necessary coins required for solving the problem. Instantly, the project was made better.

Students would write a sentence such as "I bought a boat. It cost seventeen cents," using inventive spelling, capitalization, and punctuation. Then they would draw the boat and copy and paste clip art coins next to a small clip art purse. (Obviously, we didn't worry about the actual value of items!)

I wondered if doing this exercise with real coins would accomplish the same thing. But, in discussions with teachers, they liked the idea of the abstraction of the "coins" and the open-endedness of the students' writing a problem and solving it any way they wanted with the "coins."

We did this lesson twice, once each week over a two-week period. The first time the kids made easy problems requiring only one coin, such as

"I bought a dog for one cent," and "I bought a town for five cents." They didn't have to make realistic purchases. But the next week, after learning more about coins and amounts, they created more complicated problems using multiple coins, sometimes copying and pasting additional pennies: "I bought a bunny for twenty-seven cents" and "I bought a beanie baby for seventy-two cents."

Have older students make change. For example, they can write a question like this: "If I had fifty cents, how much change would I get back if I bought a pack of gum for twenty-seven cents?"

Figure 5-1 Coins Project Example

Project: Pie Recipes

Writing recipes is an excellent project for teaching math and writing. For many years, second graders created pumpkin pie recipes for a book that was photocopied and sent home. They wrote and rewrote with pencil and paper until the basic format met the teacher's approval (crust ingredients, filling ingredients, and directions). They explored basic measurements in class (tablespoon, teaspoon, and cup) and ingredients (pumpkin, sugar, and butter).

The typical recipes were pretty funny:

Pie Filling:

    3 cups of butter

    2 tablespoons of pumpkin

    1 egg

    2 scoops of cream

    4 pounds of vanilla juice

Pie Crust:

    2 egg whites

    4 cups flour

    a pinch of salt

Directions:

    Get a bowl.

    Mix the ingredients together.

    Scoop the ingredients into the pie pan.

    Put it in the oven.

    The oven has to be up to 23 degrees.

    After it's cooked you take it out.

    Then cut the pie.

    Then eat the pie.

Because the writing and rewriting was time-consuming, this project was a natural for word processing. Over a few weeks, the students entered and corrected their information. Instead of having to rewrite each time, they edited their existing file. If they'd left out any directions or ingredients, it was easy to go back and add the information.

In addition to learning how to edit their work on a word processor, they had plenty of time to explore division using the / (slash) symbol, which has pretty much replaced the horizontal fraction bar due to the influence of computers.

Of course, this idea is not limited to pumpkin pie. Students can create any recipe—a favorite that Mom or Dad makes, ethnic foods (different recipes for each student), other holiday themes, and healthy foods. Every student can create a decidedly different recipe, and you can combine the recipes into a cookbook if you like.

Remember That It's Just a Tool

You can be sure that software and even computer hardware will be very different in just five years. Focus your lessons on educational goals so your project ideas will work no matter how everything changes.

Project: Venn Diagrams

The next project is fun and best done in pairs. Having enough computers for everyone doesn't mean students should work alone!

When your students are studying how to sort and classify information, create Venn diagrams on the computer. What I love about this idea is how many grade levels it can span—from kindergarten through adult.

Creating Venn diagrams on the computer requires little instruction from the teacher. Yet students are very involved, combining computer skills and the process of sorting and classifying objects. All that is required is basic instruction on how to open a file, draw circles, place graphics or stamps, and type some words. All of these are great computer skills, and easy to demonstrate.

Basic Venn Diagrams

Using a drawing program with premade graphics, clip art, or stamps (or kids can draw pictures), ask kids to draw two intersecting circles. (Young kids can start with one circle and advanced classes can tackle three.) Have children create their own categories or provide categories for them to choose from—animals that can walk, animals that can fly, things with eyes, round things, carnivores, and herbivores.

Figure 5-2 Venn Diagram

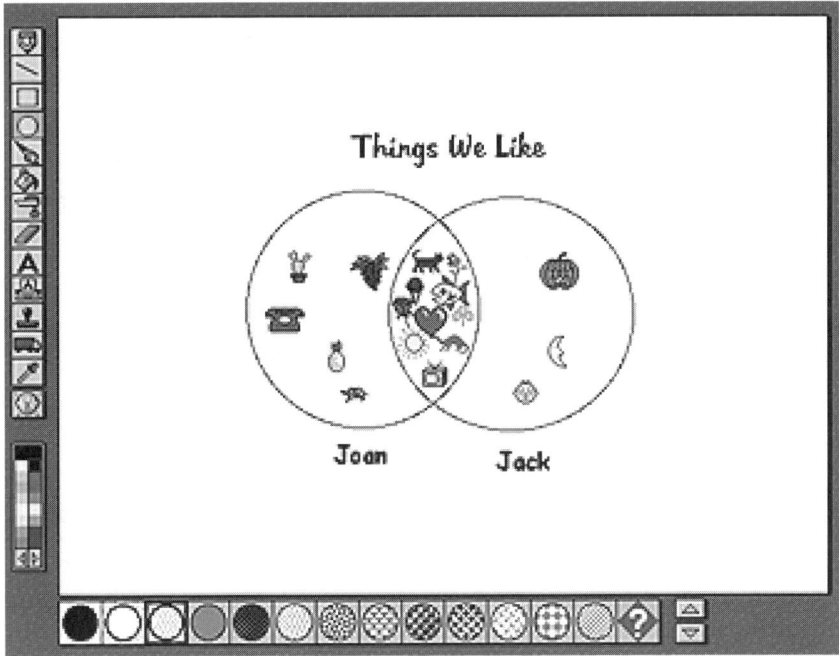

One of my favorite variations is to pair students and have them each label one circle with their name (e.g., "Things James likes" intersecting with another circle labeled "Things Caroline likes"). Of course, things both children like go in the intersection of the circles.

I always hear the sweetest conversations between partners. "Do you like cats, James?" "Me, too." "Do you like clouds?" "Not too much." "Okay, I'll just put them in my circle." "What do you think about chocolate ice cream?" They decide together where to place pictures and sometimes giggle over silly clip art. This project is also a fun way for students to get to know each other.

But what are kids learning?

The children are learning set theory and how to draw circles that intersect, which is not an easy task. If you haven't done this yourself, try it! It's a great lesson in trial and error. Computers have an EDIT:UNDO feature, so mistakes are easy to correct. Whatever you do, don't give in and draw circles for them. They will protest, at first, but they will catch on. If you want them to draw perfect circles, remind them to hold down the shift key as they draw. The children are also making labels, using a writing tool, selecting clip art or stamps, classifying objects, and creating categories.

When my second graders choose their own categories, very often a set is something like "Things Jimmy thinks are cool" and "Things that are red." What happens then is that many items in the stamp or clip art set are neither red nor cool, in Jimmy's mind, so he ends up with lots of stuff scattered outside of the intersecting circles. But that's okay. That's where these things belong.

Of course, it's sometimes hard to stop kids from adding too many pictures. Their screens quickly become overwhelming messes. But I figure that the learning went on mainly in their heads, and the printed version is only the final picture. Use other kids' examples that are easier to see (with more white space) if you want to discuss Venn diagrams with the students later on.

Being able to make changes easily is one of the great advantages of using computers. The only drawback is that it can be too easy; some kids seem to have a hard time completing any assignment. On the computer they might be creating a work of art. You watch their progress as you cruise around the room. Suddenly you return and their screens are blank! "What happened to your work?" you ask.

"I didn't like it so I erased it," they reply.

Ack, you think, but it's their choice.

Challenging Venn Diagrams

Ask students to choose categories first (e.g., "Things that are cold," and "Things you can eat"). Have them draw two intersecting circles, write their category names above the circles, and fill the circles with pictures. Then have them erase the category names, leaving a blank line (an underline) for someone to fill in later. Now have students switch pictures and try to figure out what the categories are or display the pictures on a large monitor and problem solve as a class.

This project provides a great way to talk about strategies for solving problems. Kids have to think backwards to figure out what the original categories were.

Project: Patterns

Original Patterns

Have kids create their own patterns by placing pictures (stamps or clip art) in a patterned sequence such as *ab ab* or *aa aa* or *aba aba* or *aab aa aab aa* (or whatever patterns they are learning). Have them repeat the sequence twice and then leave two blank lines for someone else to complete the pattern.

Instead of using pictures, kids could use the polygon tool (square, circle, and rectangle). They can pick patterns to fill the polygon, make regular polygons with equal sides or perfect circles, and make a pattern sequence with shapes. Around Valentine's Day, they can draw hearts and fill them with different patterns. In this way, kids draw with the polygon tool, practice copying and pasting, work with patterns, and employ the shift key to make regular polygons.

Frog Pond Patterns with Extra Lily Pads

If you remember an old program called *The Pond*, this may sound familiar.

Figure 5-3 Patterns Example

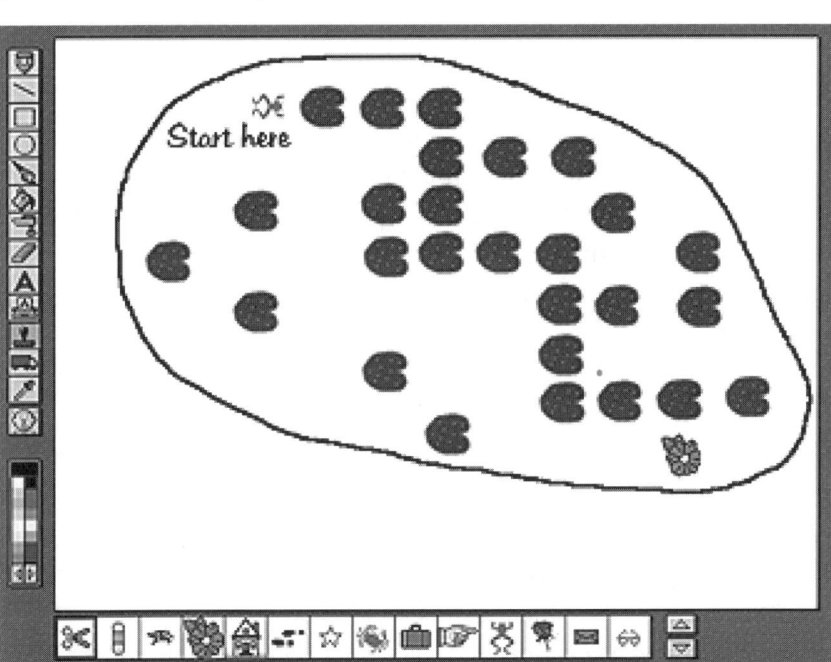

Kids have to look at the lily pads on a pond and find a pattern so that they, as a frog, may leap in a patterned way safely across the pond.

Kids can make their own ponds in a drawing program, and then trade their patterns.

The object is for students to start with a big circle (the pond). Then, they can draw a basic lily pad and copy and paste it as many times as needed.

For example, one student can create a pattern like this: three lily pads moving horizontally to the right, and then two lily pads moving vertically down from the last lily pad. This pattern should repeat over and over to fill the pond. This is the main path. After the path pattern is drawn, the student can throw in some extra lily pads (distracters) to confuse the other player.

Use Computers for Editing, Storing, and Transmitting Data

Computers are best when you need to erase or edit your work easily, communicate quickly across distances, and present, store, or search through large amounts of data. Computers combined with the Internet give us access to up-to-the-minute information (text, pictures, sounds, and movies).

One great new tool is the digital camera, which takes high quality photographs and saves them as computer graphics files. You can easily and quickly copy these files to a computer, and edit or copy and paste the images. Digital cameras let us capture kids in action without the time and expense of standard film processing. The possibilities of portfolio assessment using digital cameras are huge. And because digital storage space is getting cheaper and cheaper, it's possible to hang on to student work done on the computer.

Project: Digital Cameras and Math Activities

We had one digital camera for a campus of 850 kids. This actually worked well for a while since teachers used the camera only sporadically. Then one teacher started finding ways to use it all of the time. She finally got her own camera, but along the way she introduced the rest of us to the tool's possibilities.

For example, we encourage kids to write across the subject areas, and we know how well students have understood a concept if they are able to retell what happened. This is no easy task, especially with math. But we found that a digital camera can make the process easier.

One day, a second-grade teacher, Peggy Cling, came running into the lab to see if the camera was available. She ran back to her classroom and snapped pictures of her students doing a math activity with manipulatives. She came back with the camera, printed the pictures on lined paper, and returned to her classroom with the pictures.

The kids were putting away the manipulatives they had used to complete the math activity—from strings and objects to create Venn diagrams to different kinds of beans to sort and create pictographs. Instead of ending the activity there, Peggy presented them with pictures taken only minutes before of them doing the activity on the carpet or at their desk.

With these pictures in hand, students were asked to use the computer to write about what they did. The reinforcement of the picture kept the activity fresh in their minds, and they were able to write much more than ever before.

Kids wrote things like this: "I'm making a Venn. The Venn asks if you like school, if you have a dog, and if you like pizza. Lots of kids like pizza but not too many have dogs. Nine people like school and pizza and have dogs!"

Project: Pen Pal Letters

After kids have written a few letters to pen pals, take their pictures (either scan them or use a digital camera). Import the photos into a word processing program, and have the children type their letter below the picture. This simple addition to their letter not only motivates the kids to write more but allows their pen pals to see their correspondents.

Project: Shape Ideas

Reinforce basic concepts about shapes without wasting paper! Most, but not all of these projects use digital cameras as well. You can print any of these above projects for individual students or pull together all of the pictures into a slideshow or book.

Shape Book

Have kids draw pictures and create a book using only one shape (e.g., a circle). The pictures for a circle book might include a snowman, a sun, a doorknob, a tire, a wheel, and an eyeball. A square book could feature a checkerboard, a hopscotch game, a present, and an apartment building. You may need to show kids how to make perfect circles or squares (usually by holding down the shift key as they draw).

Find Shapes in Pictures

Have kids look for shapes in day-to-day life. Once kids start finding them, they'll see shapes everywhere.

Scan photographs from recent field trips, take photos of the playground with a digital camera, or copy interesting photos and illustrations from the Internet. Ask kids, working in pairs, to find as many hexagons, circles, and trapezoids as they can in each picture and trace them on the computer in a bold color using a drawing tool.

Robots and Polygon Drawings

Assign three or four shapes (circles, hexagons, squares, and so on) to students and have them make robots (or cars or buildings) using only these shapes.

Shape Walk

Our kindergarten students were studying shapes. Their teacher, Joanne Oppenheimer, took them on a walk in the neighborhood. The kids were to look for shapes around them. When someone, for example, found a hexagon shape in a stop sign, she'd hoist the child up near the sign. The child would point to it and another child would take a picture with the digital camera. Back in class, the child would write the word *hexagon* on the screen near the digital picture and then decorate the extra space on the screen with other hexagon pictures.

Project: Current Events and Class Newspapers

Take advantage of the up-to-date information on the Internet. Many newspapers are published on-line. Have kids follow a single topic for one or two months. Give them time each day to go on-line and find an article or picture they like. At the end of the period the children can write a summary of what they've learned.

All summaries can be combined and put into a class newspaper folder. Kids can then copy and paste articles, laying out the newspaper any way they like.

Kids can easily follow the same topic in two politically different periodicals. What are differences they see? Similarities? Can they see where some magazines are slanted, unfair, or leaving out information?

Project: Primary Source Materials, Clip Art, and Colonial America

With the explosion of information accessible to us now, I think it's important to encourage students to think about the information, its source, and the accuracy and the reliability of both. History/social studies classes are a perfect forum for this discussion. While most people think of clip art as tacky, clip art can include high-quality photos, engravings, and drawings you can find on the Internet.

Fourth graders viewed downloaded pictures (found on the Internet) in a word-processor document and were asked questions: "How old do you think this picture is? What makes you think that it's that old? What do you think is going on in the picture? Who took the picture, and why? What did they want you to think when you looked at the picture?"

Remember to ask questions specific to the pictures: "Why is the man not smiling?" "Do you think people always wore fancy clothes like theirs?" This approach encourages students to examine information with more than a cursory glance.

Even more interesting would be to provide a picture or a copy of an original document, such as the Declaration of Independence (http://www.nara.gov/exhall/charters/declaration/decmain.html). Ask students to make a list of questions they have about it and have them try to answer these questions as a class using books, on-line resources, interviews, and so on.

During a unit on Colonial America, we had no clip art to embellish the students' written projects. So the class went on-line in search of clip art, looking at sites the librarian and I directed them to. We pulled together a class clip art file. Not only did kids use this, but several teachers heard about it and asked for copies.

Of course, you need to teach students about the meaning and importance of copyright and giving credit to the original author. A great way to avoid the issue is to visit the National Archives (http://www.nara.gov). Their Web site is packed with excellent public domain pictures and documents from U.S. history. Another site is Archiving Early America (http://earlyamerica.com). It has less information but is easier for kids to search through. We found great pictures to illustrate fifth-grade colonial newspapers. Much that is available via the Web could be used to get kids thinking about certain periods and examining why some documents are important.

Use Computers for Assessing and Supporting Different Learning Styles

Project: Digital Portfolios

Many schools are moving to student evaluation through portfolio assessment, so hang on to electronic work your students make. Allow them to build a portfolio over the years. Let them select favorite examples, whether it's a piece of writing, an illustration, or a song, and put it in digital format.

Digital storage space is cheap and getting cheaper. Either save the portfolio pieces to disk or create simple Web pages. Better yet, build a school archive that will endure so students can look back on their work when they become adults. Not every school has the storage space to keep an archive, but many do. Don't assume you need to erase old work; wait until you actually need to.

Project: A Typical School Day Web Page

Make a class Web page using text, drawings, and pictures that show a typical school day. Take digital or regular camera pictures throughout one school day. Use one picture per Web page, and then have kids write a sentence or more about that picture. The classroom Web page gives you a chance to show quick snapshots of activities that happen during the day that many parents never hear about or see (gym class, snack time, recess, music class, and so on).

Creating a Web page can be simpler than you think, particularly if you use a simple page-building program such as Claris *Home Page* or Microsoft *Front Page*.

Or you can build it for free, using any text editor, if you type in the HTML commands (called "tags") by hand. This can be tedious, however. For a free, up-to-date list of HTML tags, visit the "Barebones Guide to HTML" Web site (http://www.werbach.com/barebones).

To view your page on the Internet, you will need to place it (and any graphic files you include) on a computer "server" connected to the Internet. Ask your school computer technician for details. You can also view the page in-house by simply opening the file with any Web browser, though people outside of the school won't be able to view it. This is a good way to preview it.

Project: The Year-in-Review Web Site

Figure 5-4 A Year in Review

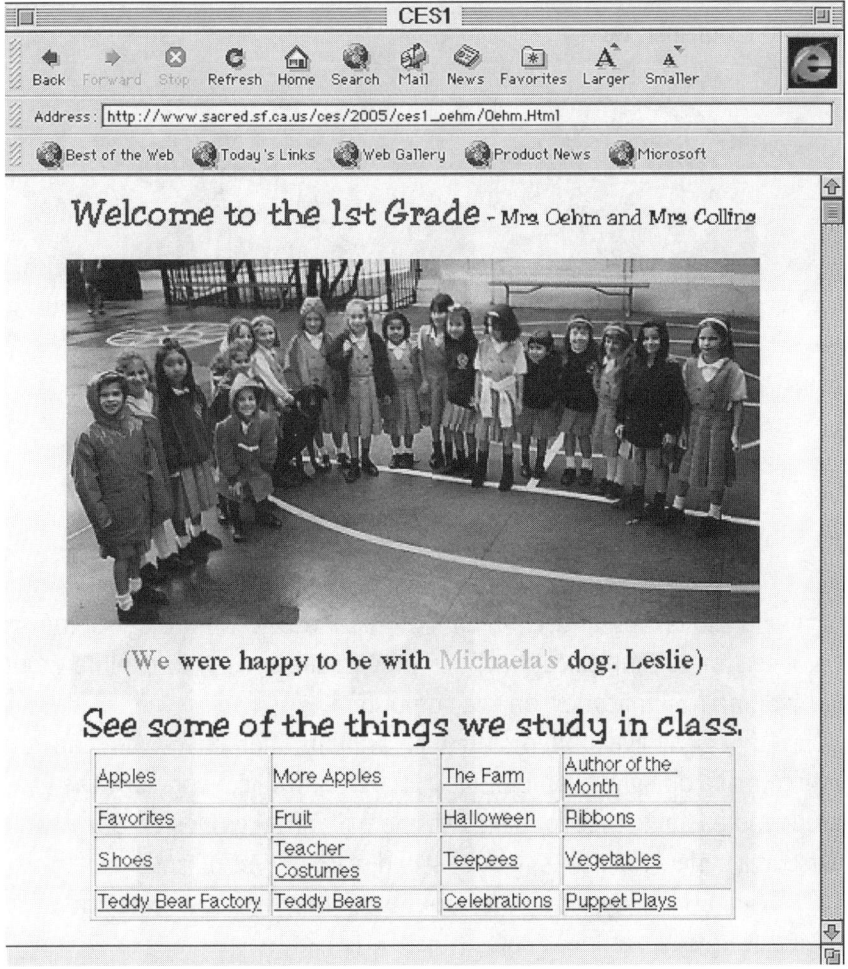

Build simple Web pages for your class throughout the year—field trip summaries, special events, science experiments, plays and performances, and guest speakers. At an end-of-the-year parent night, have the Web site accessible as a summary of what kids have learned. Get lots of input from students about what they want to have on their class "page." Let each child shine by being sure to include a wide variety of class activities and student interests. Imagine kids looking back ten to twenty years from now at the pages they created in your class!

Project: Multiple "Zoos" and Grouping

Figure 5-5 Multiple Zoo

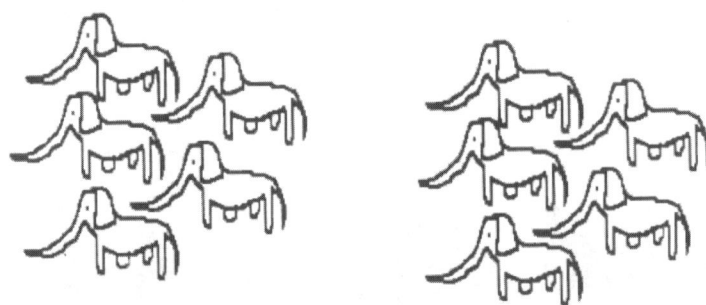

There are two groups of five elephants in the zoo. 2x5=10

It's always interesting to see which kids "get" the concept of grouping and how it relates to multiplication. This project allows kids to explore grouping by doing multiplication on the computer.

To begin, have students draw an animal. Then have them copy and paste to make one group of four. Next, have them select and copy the group of four and paste it twice to make two more identical groups of four. This, of course, is a perfect example of grouping and math. It's even hands-on, in a way.

Then ask children to write about what they've done. One boy wrote, "I see three groups of four zebras ($3 \times 4 = 12$)."

Some kids will want to keep pasting the first animal over and over until they reach twelve. You'll notice what they're doing because the pictures won't appear in groups of four.

Project: Books of 100

Figure 5-6 Book of 100 Example

The one-hundredth day of the school year was approaching, and the first graders were learning to count by groups of ten. At first, we teachers thought they could draw ten things ten times. Drawing is a necessary skill but not one we needed to focus this lesson on. Instead we had the students draw one thing, copy and paste it to make a group of ten, and then copy and paste the group ten times to make one hundred.

Every time I introduce this project to children, I am reminded of the magic of computers. The ability to select a picture and paste it repeatedly is indeed amazing. And kids find other extensions I never would imagine, like making a border around newspapers by copying and pasting one picture over and over, or copying a photo of one student's head and pasting it atop the bodies of the other students in a class photo (see page 62 for a project on image manipulation).

The classroom teacher, Liz Van Loon, and I ended up designing a project to include capitalization, periods, inventive spelling, and drawing and editing (copying and pasting). We made books of one hundred from ten pages of ten things each.

As in most projects when students must learn multiple steps, they worked more effectively in pairs. Each pair opened a simple template, a ready-made form with the outline of the finished document set up (see

Templates: You Start It, the Kids Finish It in Chapter 11 for more details). The template included a space for writing a sentence and lots of room to draw.

After typing in the sentence "I have ten lions," students drew the first lion, selected it, and then copied and pasted it. They would paste the lion eight more times to make a total of ten lions. After doing this a few times, the children had it down pat and actually enjoyed the magic of copying and pasting. Some kids asked, "After I paste one more lion and have two, can I copy those two lions and paste them four more times to make ten lions?" "Wow! Of course!" Again, kids unexpectedly took the project to a higher level than I had ever anticipated.

We printed these books in a tiny (1.5" by 2.5") format. The children loved the idea of little books, and we saved lots of paper. We printed in black-and-white, and kids colored them later.

Like many projects, the Books of 100 improved over the years.

Project: Food Groups

Another teacher varied the previous project to create a different template. The template had a title page that read "Food Groups by _____."

The following pages read: "I have one ___," "I have two ___," "I have three ___," and so on.

At the bottom of each page were the names of the food groups: fruit, vegetable, dairy, and meat. Each pair of kids made their own book that contained one page per food group. For the dairy group, one pair wrote, "I have three cheeses."

The children drew one slice of cheese, and then copied and pasted it to make the other two.

Project: Collective Nouns

When students are exploring collective nouns (e.g., a pod of dolphins, a swarm of bees, and a herd of camels), have them write the sentence, draw one of the animals, then copy and paste it enough times to make a den, bevy, or gaggle. A good example is "The army of ants marched toward the picnic table."

Project: Animated Life Cycles

One way to see if kids understand a sequence is to have them animate it. Animation is a great way to illustrate processes such as food chains, plant growth, butterfly development, the water cycle, chicks hatching, seasons changing, moon cycles, and so on. While animation seems like a very flashy, high-end type of project, it's actually very simple and powerful. The kids are really just drawing a sequence of pictures to illustrate a process.

Kids can easily create animations demonstrating any sequence of events, and they love to do it. There are many methods to get the job done: flipbooks, *KidPix, Hyperstudio,* and even the "print preview" feature in a word processor (put one picture per page at the top, and then click the next button in "print preview").

Sixth-grade students animated the ways in which caves and glaciers were formed. They drew a picture, copied and pasted it, and altered the copy to show the next stage. When they completed the drawings, they added short sentences to describe each drawing.

It was interesting to watch forty of these, although the teacher and I agreed that next time there should be four or five topics (instead of just one) for the class to animate. Seeing each sequence ten times would have reinforced the lesson just as well as seeing it forty times.

Most interesting was seeing who really grasped the concept completely. Some kids were distracted by the silliness and showed people being swallowed up by glaciers (impossible, of course). Other kids included facts about the acidity of rain and its effect on caves. Kids' misconceptions, as well as their level of understanding, became clear.

Of course, many ideas can be taught with animation. Another class demonstrated the routes that explorers took by mapping the individual explorers' courses around the world. What struck me most was the consistency with which crews either mutinied or died from scurvy!

Chapter 6
Learn from Your Students

Watch your students to determine whether a project is working. Do they get excited? Are they busy talking to each other or asking you if they can do something a little bit differently? Or conversely, do they finish too fast? Do they just do what you say and stop? Instead of telling them what to do in a project, present a problem and let them solve it in different ways. Look for something they can add. Ask yourself how they can contribute. Students shouldn't feel these projects just give them a chance to repeat an old solution to an old problem.

You can also learn computer skills from the kids. I had worked with a classroom teacher for a few years. She and I had planned some terrific stuff for her students: biographies that included a solid word-processing and editing component, projects about states with an emphasis on presentation skills and visual design, and so on. She knew what would work with her students and made good use of their time.

After two years of this, she attended our weeklong summer technology institute during which I gave a quick demonstration on how teachers could use a word processor. After she had been seated for a few minutes, I asked if she had any questions, because she hadn't started. She looked at me blankly and said, "I have no idea how to begin." I had to hold her hand as she held the mouse and show her how to use it.

Although she had been great at directing her students and creating good projects, she had no idea how to use the computer herself. In fact, she had never touched a keyboard or mouse. I was stunned and thought I had failed in those years we worked together, but later I realized that it didn't matter if she knew the technical ins and outs. She knew what was most important: how her students learned and how to design projects for them that had lasting benefits.

Project: Navajo Rugs and Symmetry

Computers are great for teaching symmetry. I love hearing kids in the early grades use the proper vocabulary when they ask to make more "pictures using lines of symmetry." This project evolved from another suggestion by a student.

For years, we had students draw meaningless symmetrical designs. One day, a student asked if the class could draw pictures instead of designs. None of us had thought of this, and I initially thought the idea would be too difficult. But when we tried it, the children were more involved in their projects and saw the need for using different lines of symmetry to achieve the right effect.

Some drawing programs (e.g., *KidPix* or *MacPaint*) have a symmetry tool; when you draw in one place, it automatically draws a mirror copy, which lets you create symmetrical pictures. Even if your program doesn't have this feature, most will let you copy a drawing, and then flip it vertically or horizontally. Sometimes kids can choose to have a vertical, horizontal, or diagonal line of symmetry for their pictures.

One November, students were studying Native Americans and looking at Navajo rugs. We decided they would draw these rugs, which are symmetrical in design, on the computers. A student would draw one fourth of a rug first, using colors common to Navajo rugs and re-creating their typically angular designs. To finish the rug, the students needed to copy, paste, and rotate, flip, or transform the image three different ways to form the complete rug.

We transferred the images into a running slideshow and shared them with the class. The students loved it, and they learned about Navajo rugs, symmetry, rotation tools, and copying and pasting all in one forty-five-minute session.

This idea can be used in all grade levels. Good subjects for symmetrical drawing include symmetrical leaves, Easter eggs, kaleidoscope views, insects, snowflakes, and self-portraits.

Project: Maps and Stamps

Figure 6-1 Map Example

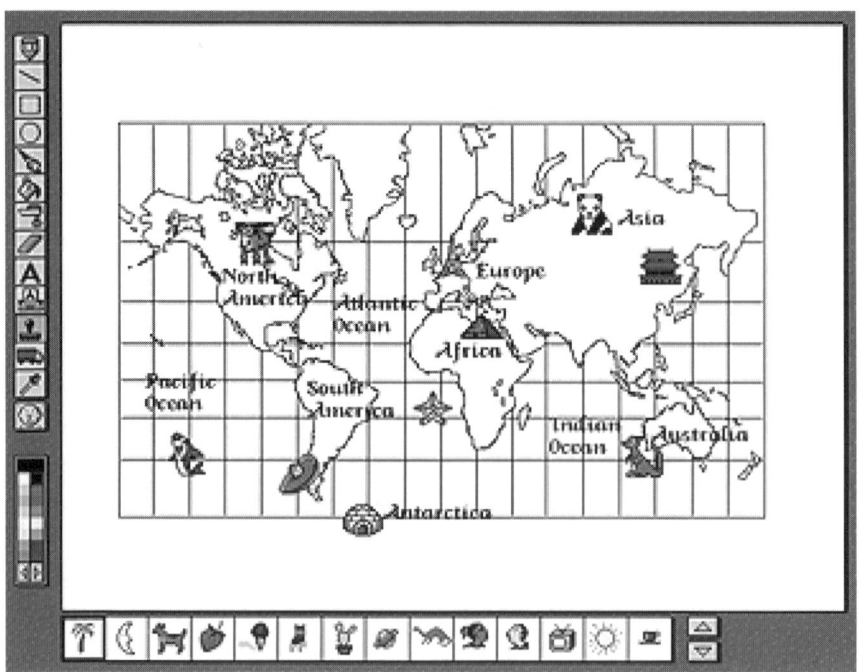

It's still difficult to find good geography software. So, following an example set by high school teacher Jean Murphy, whose students were having a hard time remembering the different place names of ancient Greece, we began scanning outlines of that empire and had students label the cities. You can apply this to any country, state, or city, of course. Today, free maps and clip art are available on the Internet if you want to skip the often tedious task of scanning.

We asked third graders first to label the world's seven continents and three major oceans. They could then color in the water and land when the labeling was finished. I thought this was a pretty good project. Unexpectedly, however, the kids finished in about ten minutes! One team asked if they could use the stamps available in the drawing program. I usually say "no" to stamps when I want students to push themselves as illustrators. But this time, with thirty minutes remaining and some students still finishing, I said, "Okay, but no more than five stamps!" I thought the kids would merely decorate the map.

Instead, I passed by later and overheard, "Ann, where do you think the pyramid belongs?"

Ann replied, "I think it's in Africa, but what part?"

The students turned my tame project of map labeling into a complex geography exercise. They were talking around the computer (my favorite thing to see) and trying to figure out where stamps belonged, rather than randomly dropping them on the map as if they were meaningless decorations.

"Where does the moose go?" one said. "How about the sombrero?" said another.

I almost didn't listen to my students; what a loss that would have been. The kids created one of the best lessons ever.

One year, we tried this project on our own state of California during a year of floods and fires. Students added pictures of flames in the southern part of the state and rain clouds in the north, as well as the labels we required: the names of the capital and largest cities, rivers, lakes, and neighboring states.

Chapter 7
Accept a Little Chaos

Computer labs and centers shouldn't be quiet places. If kids are involved and discussing their work, they will make some noise. Their final projects will be all the richer for it.

Sometimes my lab seems chaotic to the unaccustomed observer or to teachers dropping in to check their e-mail. Sometimes I think so too, but when I eavesdrop on students I'm almost always reassured that they are talking about their work and nothing else. Sometimes they get animated. They laugh and gesture. They aren't always sitting on their stools. They may be bouncing in their seats or standing. But they are always working.

Of course, an occasional "please use quiet voices" (that terrible teacher phrase) may be needed if another class is sharing the space and receiving instruction. But try to allow the volume to be a notch higher than it is in a traditional, noncomputer classroom.

 Dealing with Lost Work

Besides technical problems, losing work is the most common distraction during computer class. What should you do if student work is lost? It depends on the situation. Some options:

1. Give them extra time to make it up.
2. Tell them, "It's easier the second time."
3. Have them join a student in progress and finish together.
4. Back up student files occasionally.
5. Teach them how to make backups.
6. Copy another student's file, in progress, and have the student finish it.

Letting Students Choose

Once kids know how to use a few programs, let them make decisions about how to best communicate an idea. They could start an e-mail chain letter, write an essay, draw a picture, create a Web scavenger hunt, write and illustrate an idea, present information orally, create a slideshow, make a posterboard session, design a Web page, and so on.

Not only will this range of activities add some variety to presentations, it also lets kids tap into their own learning styles and expertise. And it puts decision-making power into their hands.

Whether kids present their ideas to each other in class or internationally via the Web, it gives other students different perspectives on how kids learn. When one child in a class really grasps a concept, he or she can share it with those not "getting" it. Kids that haven't been "getting" it might have some insight into how that student is understanding and learning. Of course, the more that kids can explore together using the computer, the more they learn from one another and gain control of their own learning.

Chapter 8 — Team Up Your Students

Never miss an opportunity to have students work together on computers. Early on, teachers thought computer work would be isolating. It doesn't have to be, and you can prevent that.

It's possible to use computers in an isolating way, especially if each student uses his or her own laptop. But writing by hand is even more isolating, if you look at it that way. Well-designed projects create more collaboration than a traditional classroom offers, which is why some chaos is normal, and even preferable.

Have Kids Teach Kids

One of my favorite teaching tricks is to have kids teach kids. Pick one of the many volunteers you're sure to have to demonstrate individual computer techniques as you talk about the project. The volunteer controls the mouse, the keyboard, and the computer. This works for several reasons:

1. If you're not being clear, you'll know immediately.
2. If no one else "gets" it, there will at least be two of you in the room that do. The student can help now, too. Just as there are

busy beavers, line leaders, and students-of-the-day, now you can appoint a computer whiz.

3. The kids can teach each other. Once you train an "expert," have that sudent train the next "expert." Then, have that student expert train the next, and so on.

Project: Peer Editing and E-mail

With e-mail and Web sites, the concept of objective peer editing is now practical for the first time. Not only can students have feedback from a teacher or friend, but also an anonymous e-mail pen pal (what I call a "Key pal") can review their work objectively. This key pal knows nothing about them and is only looking at their words. Finding key pals, as you would have selected pen pals, needs to be safely arranged ahead of time. I find teachers seeking key pals for their classes by looking online, at conferences, or among my teacher school buddies.

The most important point for the children to understand is that the mechanics of editing words on a computer are simple. They should be able to give someone their rough draft, take the changes suggested, and make them (if they want)—without worrying about reentering all of the text again.

 Let Kids Collaborate

Project: Electric Songs

My first idea for a collaborative project that really gelled was creating electric "songs." This happened after my second year teaching with computers. Of course the idea developed over time, but the kindergarten teacher and I started by assigning one line of a song (about the animals on grandmother's farm) to each pair of students. They drew a picture of their lyric and typed it on the screen.

We put the song together in a slideshow program that allows you to add sounds and had the students sing their lines. Each student had to draw, write, and sing his or her phrase, and then listen to the entire slideshow. Talk about reinforcing a concept!

This project took very little preparation and follow-up. The students learned to draw and write on the computer, and they discovered how sounds were added—a relatively advanced bit of multimedia. Everyone had fun and learned.

Have the children draw first so they don't accidentally erase the lyrics. It can also take the young ones awhile to type the lyrics.

This project doesn't require a lot of preparation time, but preparation from all teachers involved makes all of the difference. Again, good teaching leads to good computer projects, never the other way around.

On one occasion, this project failed when students were supposed to illustrate a song about types of clouds. Before demonstrating the computer skills, I asked them if they'd enjoyed learning the cloud song, and I saw only blank faces. Their teacher had neglected to prep them, despite promising to do so. So that first lesson they illustrated the first line of the song (which I taught them) out of context, knowing very little about clouds. Naturally, they needed lots of guidance.

A week passed before they returned to finish the project, and I thought they would catch up in that time. I certainly understand how "busy" things can get, but the children showed up the next week still not having sung the song.

We started adding their singing to the project, anyway. Despite some valiant efforts by kids trying to fake it, the only person you could really hear singing was the teacher! Even a little preparation can make all the difference.

Project: Truck Stacks

Several years ago, my school built a new gym. There was construction and lots of noise during the day.

The kindergarten teacher took advantage of the situation. We checked out some books from the library with pictures of the different machines being used in construction—land movers, cement trucks, plows, tractors, and so on. We scanned in the pictures and put each one on a *Hypercard* "page" with a text area for kids to write in.

The fourth graders came to the computer lab with their kindergarten "buddies." Each fourth grader's task was to type in the buddy's name and whatever the kindergartner had to say about the picture. The younger student would then draw on top of the scanned image, adding people, dirt, a sun, and so on.

Then the teacher took a small tape recorder and recorded the sounds of the machines at work. As it turned out, the machines all sounded the same.

Instead of using the repetitive, loud, grinding sounds from eight of the fifteen or so machines, we recorded the kids' voices imitating the sounds they had heard. The kids made sounds ranging from a whir to a clunk-clunk to a loud screech.

The kindergartners loved the one-on-one attention from older students, the older kids learned some skills in "teaching," the little kids had a gentle introduction to drawing on the computer, and everyone had fun.

Project: City Guide

Students in our third grade study their city and local area. After exploring local tourist attractions, they choose a favorite, draw a picture of it on the computer, and word process a short paragraph trying to interest tourists in visiting their particular site. Here's an example:

> Visit Lombard Street. It has eight to ten curves and is made out of cobblestones. It is the crookedest street in the whole wide world. You can walk down or up, but you can't drive up only down because it is too steep to go up. Wear sneakers if you walk down. You could run, too.

Chapter 9   *Have Fun*

I usually try to add some kind of zing to every project to make it more silly or fun, such as scanning real pictures of coins instead of drawing them or finding clip art illustrations. This doesn't erase the educational value of a project, but it can make the whole process more enjoyable for you and your students. (Between busy schedules, tight budgets, and computer crashes, you need to keep as much fun in your job as you can!)

Project: Digital Field Trip

Take pictures on a field trip with a digital camera and then put the pictures into a word processor or multimedia program. Create a class summary of the field trip as a way to have students rethink and relearn the ideas you explored. Parents can see it, too! You can send it home on a disk, post it to the Web, download it to a VCR tape, or show it on a parent night.

The first time I attempted this project, it was a little chaotic. Clearly, my directions were developing as we started. Sometimes this happens.

Each student had a different picture on his or her screen, with space for writing a few sentences. The kids all started writing about the *same* thing —playing with Roly-Poly bugs (also known as potato bugs) that ball up when you touch them. Apparently, this was a huge highlight of the field trip.

Students with pictures of beautiful sunsets, poppies blooming, kids splashing in water near a beach, or kids preparing meals were still writing about those darned Roly-Poly bugs.

I had to stop and ask them to write about what was going on in the picture they had on their screen. This was a different task than the usual "what did you do on vacation" question. Instead, they had to focus on one activity, remembering an important point or something memorable. Here's an example:

> In this picture, Ted and Maria are resting on the dangerous cliff sign after we hiked straight up the hill from the beach. We had to be careful not to touch any poison oak on the way up. We stopped here to have a drink and a snack.

In the future, I hope my students will have several cameras and video recorders so they can take whatever pictures they want. They might still need some direction if they all want to photograph the Roly-Poly bugs!

Project: Altered Images

The best way for kids to understand media is to create it. Once they see how easy it is to manipulate an image, they'll think twice when they see pictures in newspapers and magazines.

Scan pictures or have students take digital photos of themselves. Then ask students to "alter" them. It's best to have them change their own picture rather than someone else's!

As early as the fourth and fifth grades, show kids some easy tricks with high-end photo manipulation tools, such as PhotoShop (if you have them). Or bring in a parent who can demonstrate a similar program for the class. Otherwise, any drawing program will work. Younger kids can draw mustaches and devil horns on photos. They'll see immediately how easy it is to change hair color, blacken teeth, or put their own heads on monsters' bodies. Then you can show them some real-life examples. A good example is the *Time* and *Newsweek* cover photos (December 1, 1997) of the septuplet mom from Iowa. In one, her teeth have been corrected to help her look more attractive. The other shows her teeth as they appear in real life.

Figure 9-1 Altered Images

Project: Analogies and Scanning Hands

Scanning can be wearisome, resulting in crashing, memory problems, and connection failures. But many of us have had fun photocopying our faces and hands, and kids can do the same thing with a scanner.

Three to four kids can scan their hands simultaneously on a flatbed scanner. In this project, kids then paste the pictures of their hands into a word processor and write about them. As directed, they make analogies to rivers, plains, mountains, and valleys. One child wrote, "My hand looks like streams of water going different directions to other places."

Project: Clip Art Leaves

Kids were studying different leaf classifications, such as lobed, with teeth, and smooth. Their teacher had big bags of beautiful leaves that the kids were going to sort into groups. What could we do to reinforce or cover this topic on the computer? Being a fan of copying and pasting and clip art, I came up with the following lesson.

I took a variety of leaves from the bags. In ten minutes—with no technical problems!—I had scanned beautiful color pictures of the leaves. You could clearly see the edges of the leaves and the veins. Be careful when doing this; the scanner lid crushed several of the dried leaves. You could place paper on top of the leaves instead of the heavy lid, as a precaution.

If you don't have a scanner or leaves handy, you could go on-line and get pictures of leaves from the Internet. When you need to find something like this on-line, consider assigning it to older students as a project instead of doing the work yourself.

Using *Hyperstudio*, I made a stack of leaf scans. Kids, in pairs, picked a category of leaves. A favorite in one class was "smooth." On their template card they drew the word "smooth." Then they flipped through the clip art pages, discussing which leaves they considered to be "smooth." Finding one, they could select it, copy it, and paste it to their card. If a group finished early, I would paste another blank card to their stack for a different category.

We didn't print color copies because it would waste too much paper and ink. Instead, I combined their cards into a class stack of leaves with a transition so cards dissolved one into another. We watched the beautiful slideshow over and over.

Naturally, you can apply this concept to other science topics, such as bats, insects, spiders, cloud types, and geology (rock types).

Project: Make Animated and Noisy Spanish Cartoons

Kids love to play with the bells and whistles of multimedia software, such as adding sound and animation. Sometimes these extra features are annoying (for teachers anyway). Kids yell into the microphone for effect or add so many sounds that they overwhelm the project.

A good way to strike a balance is to allow them free rein—but in a foreign language (if they are studying one). Ask students to make a cartoon. Using something like *Hyperstudio*, they can create cards for each scene of the cartoon and draw the characters and scenery. For the dialogue, have them record their voices speaking the conversation in the foreign language or simply have them read captions out loud, live. Encourage them to be as silly and as dramatic as they like. Usually, children are more reserved in a foreign language, making this shift a natural match for sound recordings.

Project: Planet Day

For years, our school has had students who are studying the planets complete a report and share it while dressed as their planet. To give their project a different spin, we have students write a postcard from their planet (on the computer). To personalize the card, they copy and paste commemorative stamps to their postcards (see the Commemorative Postage Stamps project in Chapter 4). Here's an example:

> Hi, I'm on Venus talking with a Venutian named Mike. I miss you but like the warm weather here. We are very close to the sun! Look in the sky at night for Venus. It's one of the only planets that can be seen with the naked eye. Got to run, Mrs. Venus (the goddess of love and beauty) is making pancakes. Bye!

For the picture side of the postcard, they can draw a rendition of their planet based on pictures, or add real pictures that are scanned or from the Internet. A good bet for images is the NASA site on the Web (http://www.nasa.gov).

They can even add video clips or sounds, such as "This is Elizabeth, signing off from Venus." Kids "ooh" and "ah" each time a real picture of a planet is shown, let alone any short video clips or sounds. Of course, nothing really beats seeing the little boys and girls all dressed up in their bulky, awkward planet costumes gesturing and pointing as they talk about their planet.

To have the presentations go as smoothly as possible, assign kids to work in pairs so one student operates the computer, clicking the mouse, as the performer talks. Kids could write postcards from the Oregon Trail, the New World, or an explorer's ship.

Chapter 10

Avoid Hardware- and Software- Specific Projects

Avoid techno-lust! Magazines relentlessly hype new technology and make you want to run out and get it. If you give in, you'll spend all your time on upgrades that often don't pan out. The best educational technology is the most general—simple drawing and word-processing programs. If you design your projects for these, instead of for special tools unique to one program, upgrades won't bother you.

Focus on what you want to do, not the tools or methods used to do it. Assume anything is possible. Develop the idea first, and then worry about how to implement it.

Any project based on writing (word processing) is a great start (see page 18). You can use any word processor and any kind of computer. And you are off to a great start educationally, as well.

The Internet is another good example of something that is neither hardware- nor software-specific. You can explore it with an IBM-compatible or Macintosh computer using any one of several Web browsers. With a well-designed project, it shouldn't matter which computer or software title you use.

Creating simple Web pages doesn't take much learning beyond word processing. (See "A Typical School Day Web Page" in Chapter 5.) Most Web browsers for viewing them are free, and if your funds are limited or you're not on the Web, it doesn't matter. You can view pages that appear only on your local computer or network, not on the global Internet, by simply opening the file with any Web browser. This may help reduce security concerns, too. Or ask someone, perhaps a parent, to post final Web pages for a week on his or her Web server at work. Let everyone know the URL (Universal Resource Locator or Web site address).

The following projects are great because the skills involved—word processing, drawing, setting up page layouts, and creating links—will remain the same for some time, if not forever.

Project: Web Scavenger Hunt

Use what's already on the Internet. Ask kids what they want to know and then construct an Internet search (so it's safe). Since you're designing the hunt, you'll know that the sites the children visit have meaningful content and are age-appropriate. Later, have them create educational Web hunts for the class.

Jason Hovey, an imaginative computer lab teacher, came up with the perfect scavenger hunt for his fourth-grade students. After reading the popular novel *From the Mixed-Up Files of Mrs. Basil E. Frankweiler,* by E. L. Konigsberg (Atheneum), kids working in pairs opened a *Hyperstudio* template he had created. In it were directions:

1. Open your Web browser and go to New York's Metropolitan Museum (http://www.metmuseum.org).

2. Copy and paste a picture of the museum back to this stack.

3. If I want to find out the hours of the cafeteria in the Met, what number should I call? Copy and paste that number back to this page.

4. Now go to the "armor" page link. Copy and paste a piece of armor you like back to this stack.

More directions followed. The project was a terrific follow-up to the book the children had just read. Kids were learning how to copy and paste images and text from the Internet, using multiple programs simultaneously, and reading Web pages for content. Now they were equipped to get information from the Internet without having to print out entire sites. They could copy the parts they wanted to their own files. You could do this for any book you read.

Project: Create Graphs from Scratch

Figure 10-1 Graphs (Pictograph)

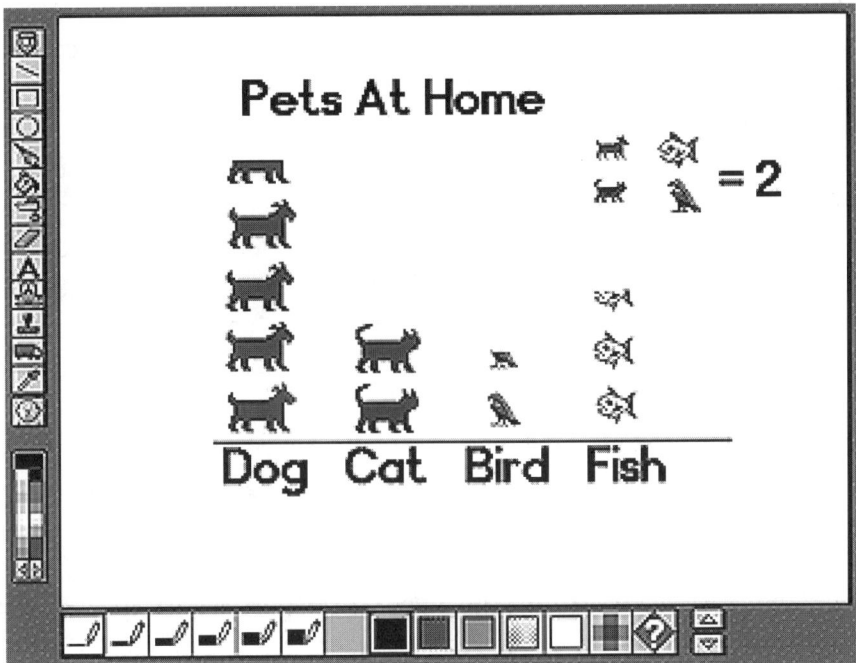

The first time I showed my students how to use electronic graphing tools to generate graphs, kids asked if they could make other graphs after they finished the required assignment. They thought it was fun. As a math teacher for many years, I'd never had kids ask if they could do *more* work!

Who would think that kids could describe making graphs as fun? I remember so much frustration when I was a student when I created fancy graphs that I ruined at the last minute by rubbing a hole through the paper with the eraser.

With computers, kids can draw graphs, teachers can guide them if they have made mistakes (such as not using a uniform scale), and students can easily make corrections until they get the project right. This is a tremendous advantage over graphing on paper, where any change requires tedious redrawing or hole-forming erasure.

There are plenty of specific graphing programs and general programs (such as *Excel*) that can create graphs automatically. But each program has different, specific techniques, and the automation prevents students from understanding how graphs are made. Instead, have students make graphs from scratch on the computer using simple drawing tools. Kids still need to go through the steps of creating graphs, so they learn about descriptive titles, categories, consistent spacing, legends or keys, and precision in giving information.

Create questionnaires and conduct surveys in person, or get fancy and solicit data from folks through e-mail or the Internet. Using any drawing program or word processor with graphics tools, have kids create graphs from scratch. Later on, when they are older and more knowledgeable, they can use the powerful graphing tools found in most current spreadsheet and database programs.

When kids get to use electronic graphing software, it's interesting to see what types of graphs they pick for different sets of data. It's a great teaching opportunity to talk about which graph type is best for things like plant growth over time—a pie chart, line graph, or pictograph? They may have made all of them, but which one makes the most sense?

Of course, you can make all of these by hand, too, and it's worth covering the most common—pie, line, and bar graphs. A great follow-up in the upper grades would be to graph the same data electronically with a computer-graphing tool. The children can compare their handmade graphs with the automatic ones.

Because changes are easy to make, kids can experiment with different graph types to see which one shows the information best. If you were teaching kids to graph with pencil and paper, that would be a teacher's nightmare—too many corrections to be made, too much time spent redrawing.

But with computer tools, kids can express their conclusions differently. They can choose different pictures for pictographs, colors, patterns, fonts, or portions of data. If they make mistakes, they don't have to start over from the beginning. They can just return to their computer file and make changes.

Project: Make a Misleading Graph

Of course, there's a great lesson in manipulation of data that comes out of this, too. If you're trying to hide the fact that teen smoking is on the rise, you might use a graph with inconsistent spacing, reversed categories, axes that don't start at zero, or the wrong graph type.

Discuss with the kids how they might recognize this kind of data manipulation. Have them read a variety of *real* graphs and check them for accuracy. (Keep an eye out for misleading graphs in the newspaper.) Demonstrate the methods, and then challenge students to make a misleading graph on the computer using drawing tools. Make sure they don't just change the numbers!

Chapter 11
Make Sure Students Do the Work, Not You

I made a discovery after I had been teaching with computers for a few years. The harder I worked on a project—carefully designing it, creating elaborate graphics and instructions—the less students learned or cared. I was killing myself with work and killing students' interest at the same time.

Suddenly, I realized that students didn't mind doing the work I hated. In fact, they loved it. The more I let them do, the harder they worked—and the more they enjoyed it. The results were often different than the pretty little pictures I had in my head when I invented the project, but they were always more interesting.

So I stopped creating elaborate projects to show how neat *I* was, and gave the students room to show how neat *they* were. This is when I really began to enjoy teaching.

How much preparation time are you spending? Can older students set the project up for a younger grade? It's not a matter of laziness; if you are spending more time prepping for a project than kids will spend working on it, you should question that project's educational value.

Ask kids what they want to learn. More specifically, ask what they want to know. It doesn't have to be about computers. If they want to learn about cars, help them find on-line pictures, automaker Web sites, e-mail addresses of car manufacturers, fax numbers, and phone numbers. Go to a car dealer and take digital pictures. Do interviews either in person or via e-mail and fax.

The key is to specify the goals of your project, not to identify every step of the method for achieving those goals. Every detail you specify is something that can go wrong as students work through the project.

In the Navajo Rugs and Symmetry project (described in Chapter 6), we had students draw one quarter of a symmetrical Navajo rug and then copy, paste, and flip or rotate the quarter three times to form a whole rug. When my colleague Joanne Oppenheimer and I were planning the project ahead of time, we tried to write explicit directions for how to first flip one way and then another, and then rotate an additional part differently. We were getting confused ourselves! Then we realized we had inadvertently created an opportunity for kids to experiment with these rotations until they could get them right! Sometimes a lot of explicit directions just aren't necessary.

Project: Templates: You Start It, the Kids Finish It

Figure 11-1a Template Example

Figure 11-1b Template Example

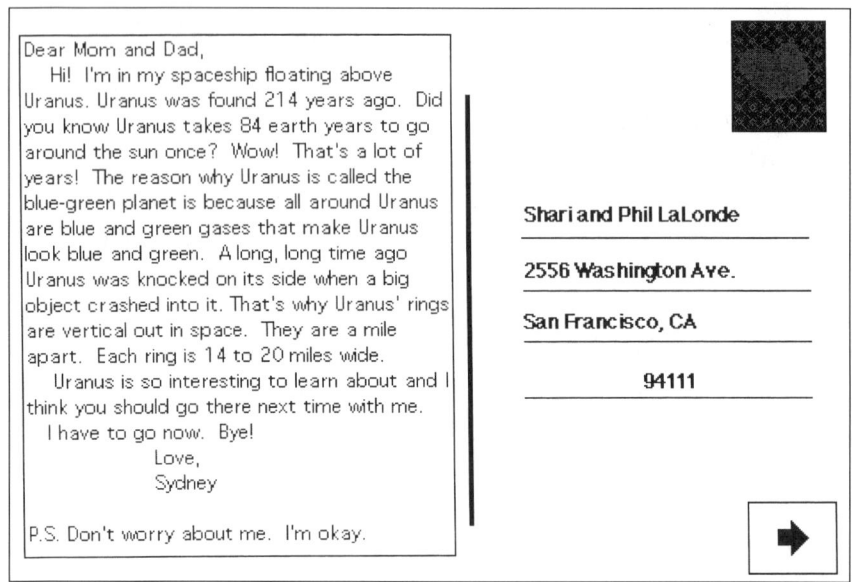

What is your goal, to teach technology or to use technology to teach? To have the students master software programs, or to produce the content for a presentation? Either goal is fine, but if you have limited time and resources, you may want to jump-start a project by creating a basic template in which students can enter their writing and drawings (see the Books of 100 project in Chapter 5).

As kids get older, they will want to personalize the template. When you have enough time and your kids are ready, have them start the project from scratch.

A basic template has one space for typing and another for illustrations. In the area for typing, set the font and style to make them easy for a student to read. Leave just enough room for the amount of text they can reasonably type at their age: one word, one sentence, several sentences, or short paragraphs. There are "school fonts" available so students can type their writing in whatever printed writing style you teach.

To create an illustration space, simply place a rectangle or square to define the area where the kids should draw. The kids I have worked with seem to like having a delineated area rather than a completely blank screen.

Once you make one complete template, copy it to each student's disk or folder, or create many numbered copies on a shared server and assign numbers to students. These templates work with any subject where you combine drawing and text, no matter how diverse: autobiographies, health stories, insect and mammal reports, mission histories, and famous women's biographies.

Project: Pack Your Suitcase!

Figure 11-2 Pack Your Suitcase

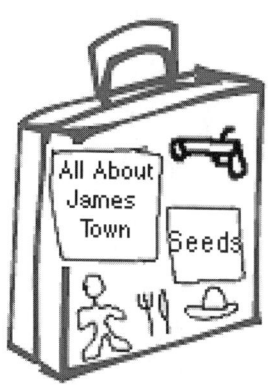

Two teachers I worked with (Diane Forsell and Marilyn Schaumburg) came up with a great idea that combines history and art. The first-grade children were studying the New World. The teachers took a picture of an empty suitcase from clip art and asked students to fill it up with pictures of what they would take on a trip to the New World if they were European adventurers.

Each student had a picture of a suitcase on his or her screen. Inside the suitcase they placed things people of all ages coming to the New World would need: guns, books, seeds, dolls, shoes, travel guides, and clothes. (Of course, there were some kids who wanted to draw roller skates, but after some reasoning they realized those didn't belong!)

This idea spawned many others. We asked, "What would you need to travel in space?"

"Chapstick so my lips wouldn't be too dry," said one student. Another said, "Oxygen so I can breathe."

We also asked, "What would you pack to visit your grandparents?"

"My favorite toy. I would bring my pillow and suitcase," wrote a student.

Chapter 12
Decide If the Computer Is the Right Tool

If using the computer doesn't make learning or teaching more effective, why use it? A computer is a great tool for some things, but not for everything. And you don't need the snazziest equipment, either. My husband drools when he sees a cordless electric drill, but a $1.99 screwdriver is usually a better tool for most household jobs.

Ask yourself, What does the computer add to the project? Don't use the computer if it bypasses necessary manual dexterity skills, such as drawing and writing, or skips important steps—graphing software that does it all for you is rarely good for kids. If you can photocopy reproductions, draw with crayons, or use pencils just as easily and effectively, do it. Remember, an important part of understanding computers is knowing when not to use them.

And don't use computers purely as mindless entertainment to keep kids busy. There are too many educational things kids can—and love—to do on computers.

Use computers to do the things the machines do best: to sort and present information, as a tool for collaboration, for students with special needs, or as a patient tutor willing to repeat things over and over, unhurriedly.

With kids in grades four and five, I've let them choose how they would like to present information: multimedia presentation, written essay, posterboard, or illustrations. Once kids have learned the basics of a few programs, let them choose the method with which they are most comfortable to present their information. Not only will they create better and more diverse projects, but they will have a chance to see information presented by their peers, who often choose different approaches that reflect their learning styles.

The more we can let kids shape their own learning, the better. It's not important that you have mastered all available software titles. Kids will help each other learn about them. You can focus your time on guiding their content learning.

Meeting Standards, Rubrics, and State Frameworks

Recently, I sent some students' work in to a multimedia competition. One of the requirements was to list the educational objectives for each project. The rules specified that objectives be pulled from local or state frameworks. So I pulled out our California State Math and Language Arts Standards for first grade to fulfill this requirement (you can often find your area's standards on-line; California's are available at http://www.cde.ca.gov/board/board.html). The International Society for Technology Education (ISTE) has a site with a good list of technology standards (http://www.iste.org).

I was quickly able to make a long list of objectives that were supported by one simple project first graders did when studying coins (see the Math Problems and Coins project in Chapter 5). They follow (numbers are listed as they appear in the standards):

Mathematics

Number Sense

1. Students understand and use numbers up to 100.

1.1 count, read, and write whole numbers to 100.

1.3 represent equivalent forms of the same number through the use of physical models, diagrams, and number expressions (to 20).

1.5 identify and know the value of coins and show different combinations of coins that equal the same value.

2. Students demonstrate the meaning of addition and subtraction and use these operations to solve problems.

2.5 show the meaning of addition (putting together, increasing).

2.6 solve addition and subtraction problems with one- and two-digit numbers (e.g., 5 + 58 = ___).

Algebra and Functions

1. Students use number sentences to solve problems.

1.1 write and solve number sentences from problem situations that express relationships involving addition and subtraction.

1.2 understand the meaning of the symbols +, -, =.

1.3 create problem situations that could lead to given number sentences involving addition and subtraction.

Mathematical Reasoning

1.2 use tools such as manipulatives or sketches to model problems.

Language Arts

Punctuation

1.5 use period, exclamation point, or question mark at the end of sentences.

Capitalization

1.7 correctly capitalize the first word of a sentence, names of people, and the pronoun "I."

Spelling

1.8 spell three- and four-letter short-vowel words and phonetically spell other sight words correctly.

ISTE Technology Literate Students (abbreviated)

1. Use input devices and output devices to successfully operate computers (mouse, keyboard, monitor, printer).

5. Work cooperatively and collaboratively with peers, family members, and others when using technology in the classroom (children work in pairs).

8. Create developmentally appropriate multimedia products (text, illustrations, and clip art).

9. Use technology resources for problem solving, communication, and illustration of thoughts, ideas, and stories.

Well-designed projects, like well-designed lessons in any content area, just *naturally* fit any set of sound educational objectives.

A few years ago I worked with my librarian to solve the problem of content-free research projects. Kids were learning lots of computer skills and could dazzle their audiences with clever multimedia presentations about science and history, with animations, and with beautiful scans, but their projects were educationally empty. Now we regularly refer to Eisenberg and Berkowitz's Big Six model for designing research projects (http://thebig6.com). Once kids know what the expectations are and have a simple rubric for grading, the projects have a better balance between information and bells and whistles. *A Teacher's Guide to Performance-Based Learning and Assessment* (Association for Supervision and Curriculum Development, 1996) is a good reference for getting started with rubrics.

 ## Avoid Adding Bells and Whistles

Don't get yourself involved in a meaningless computer project because it's the "new thing," or because your school spent the money and wants to see the equipment used. There are plenty of great things to do with computers that are more worthwhile.

One common mistake is scanning pictures unnecessarily when they would look better photocopied and glued to a sheet of paper. Another is having kids type long reports in a multimedia format. If the goal of the lesson is really editing and creative writing, leave it in a word processor. The bells and whistles just make it easy for students to get sidetracked.

Work with Parents, Not for Them

The goal of all these projects should be to educate students, not to impress parents. As tempting as it is to design something that makes parents' jaws drop, those kind of projects are rarely the most instructive.

And even if you do create a flashy multimedia show, parents may not be wowed. Remember, if they aren't familiar with computers, they'll have no idea how hard you worked.

One of our most savvy teachers was excited to develop a women's history project with her students. It started with an image the teacher had scanned of the assigned famous woman, surrounded by appealing drawings and stories students made to illustrate her life story.

The teacher took a ten-second video clip of each student dressed as "her woman." "Hi. I'm Amelia Earhart," said one. The teacher carefully digitized the video and inserted it into each girl's stack. It was a great addition. But when parents came for the students' presentations, they weren't impressed. They had no idea how much time the teacher had taken putting this special program together. Maybe she won't do it next year. The teacher put in the extra work to demonstrate her new knowledge, and her students found it fun. But the payoff for those many extra hours of work was minimal.

Some of the most complicated projects look like simple drawings. For example, when I share the Books of 100 (see Chapter 5) with prospective parents, they are nonplussed—at first. Then I explain the copying and pasting, inventive spelling, punctuation, and drawing involved and there are then sighs of "Wow" and "Can you teach us that, too?"

Nothing you do will impress parents as much as the simplest drawing by their child. Your projects should show off the student's work, not yours. And projects that do that just happen to be the most educational.

Photocopying and Scanning

More than once, a student has arrived in the computer lab with a book containing a picture she needs to scan. I begin the process of showing her how to scan the photo, save the file to disk, and print the picture. This is a minimum ten-minute task even if there aren't any technical problems (and there almost always are). While we're sitting, chatting amiably, and waiting for the scanner to inch slowly along, I think to ask, "What do you need this picture for? A computer project? To add to a word-processed document?"

"No," says the student. "I just need a copy I can glue to my poster."

The student could have photocopied the picture in seconds! And the quality would have been better.

This problem continues to haunt me—and continues to happen. It reminds me to always consider whether something could be done as effectively (and more easily) with a simpler tool.

Instead of scanning and sending files through a modem, would a fax machine be faster? Does a project really need a computer, or could it be done more efficiently with pen and paper or graphing calculators?

Use Good Old Technology

One teacher organized an archaeological dig for his students. He wanted to prepare a presentation for parents combining text with pictures taken at the "dig," and he was planning to scan sixty photographs. If you've ever done much scanning, you know that it can be very time-consuming and a memory hog to boot. Instead, another teacher happened to be hanging around and suggested we use the opaque projector instead of scanning. This is an older type of projector that can show images of any object. You place an apple on a glass panel and the image is captured by the machine above and projected onto a large screen. These used to be more available in schools, but these days they're harder to find. He saved us ten hours of work!

If the teacher needed digital photos, scanning would still be the wrong approach; a digital camera could achieve the same result much more easily. Remember, just because a project requires lots of time or uses complicated technology, that doesn't make it better!

Use Word Processing and Databases

A second-grade teacher, Janet Crooks, wanted her students to set up a database to sort class information and draw conclusions. The students conducted a survey, asking questions like these:

"What's your favorite sport?"

"What's your favorite ice cream flavor?"

"How old are you?"

"How many pets do you have?"

I thought, "How BORING!" What was she thinking? Getting second graders to sort through a database sounded like a disaster in the making, but I reluctantly went along.

As they learned how to sift the information about their classmates, I heard that special kind of commotion that successful projects spawn, and excited comments such as, "Did you know that John is the only one that likes chocolate ice cream and soccer?" and "Wow. Eileen and Jim are the only two that like basketball and have four people in their families."

Students wanted to do more and more sifting of information to see what other fascinating coincidences they could find. Other kids would try the same search, to see if Mary really was the only one who was seven, had a pet bird, and liked vanilla ice cream.

This was not a huge database lesson—I spent about thirty minutes or so with them sifting through information—but the children got the gist of why databases are important and how they can be used. If you can imagine doing this project with pen and paper, it's easy to see how computers were essential this time around.

The lesson also helped kids understand the library's electronic card catalog. It's hard to explain a database in the abstract, but practical examples bring the lesson home.

Chapter 13

What Next?

 Try Something New (Even If You're Already Busy)

Integrating computers requires more trial and error than other curricular programs you've done. I've always liked how my job is full of constant change, problem solving, and experimentation. Because I'm dealing with a new tool, I feel freer to take chances and try untested ideas. But it's not just new teachers or the folks dealing with new tools who need to keep experimenting. As my friend Carol Sauer (an extraordinary librarian) told me, "Computers are a little scary to implement, because usually you're not doing so in the privacy of your classroom where no one but you and your students know if you fail."

Don't feel you need to master a program before using it with your students. I was recently interviewing candidates for a computer-related job. One asked, "When do you learn to use new software?"

"On the fly," I replied.

Since the beginning, and to this day, I jump in with a class and learn a program as they do. Kids don't mind at all and are so proud when they can teach you something. They will be very flexible if everything goes haywire, as long as they know from the start that they are exploring the unknown with you. If things get completely out of hand and it's a waste of time without salvation, scrap the whole thing and reassure the kids that you will get back to the program at another time. Or gather the children around and ask for their feedback on what would make the program better.

If you want to try something new in a computer lab, or with a computer resource person in your room, more of your dignity may be at stake. But don't worry too much. Even the best teachers, after decades of teaching, still start dreadful projects they instantly regret.

One year a long-term substitute joined us halfway through the school year to work with teachers developing computer projects. She hopped right in and was having great success helping teachers plan new ways to use computers, even though these teachers had been using computers and electronic resources for years.

But she was surprised that even with their technical knowledge and fearlessness around new tools, some faculty members were already stuck doing the same old projects—projects that may have been innovative just a few years before. When she suggested even subtle changes, they didn't want them. It was as though they had mastered technology, implemented it, and didn't want it—or them—to change.

Don't get stuck! In technology, even 1994 is a long time ago now. And the only way to adapt is to experiment.

 Contact Me

E-mail me (elin@realchange.org) or visit my Web site (http://www.realchange.org/compideas). I will be featuring the best projects sent in by readers both on the Internet site and in my next book. Visit to see what's new or share your brainstorms!

What's on the Horizon?

Technically, who knows? You can be sure, though, that the same classic teaching principles will carry us through any new stuff that comes our way.

The key to mastering the new is the old—finding ways to communicate core subjects in incredibly efficient and fun ways using computers. Technology will only be as good as your teaching methods. It's not the tools but the teachers behind them that make them useful.

As a new parent I can't wait to do several things with my daughter when she goes to school.

1. Fax. I hope her kindergarten classroom will have a fax machine. Occasionally, she could send me something she's proud of and working on in class, or I could send her things.

2. Web Cam (a camera that sends a snapshot of the classroom to the Internet every few minutes). Hopefully, I will be able to peek into Anna's classroom occasionally to see what's going on without disturbing the class or my daughter. If I have a better sense of what's happening, I might see ways I can support her learning better at home, too.

3. E-mail. As she begins to read and write, I could e-mail her during the day with an important message or the electronic equivalent of a note tucked into a lunch bag. She could e-mail me too, to tell me (or her grandparents or cousins) about anything that excites her, or something she forgot to tell us, or to request a last-minute ride she needs to an athletic event.

Start small and simple. Have lots of fun. And take a chance!

Appendix: Basic Preparation Rules

As strange as it seems, planning is the key to good improvisation. Having the basics prepared will give you the time and confidence to take advantage of unexpected developments. Once you have everything planned it's easier to take chances, because you have something to fall back on if it fails. If you have young students, these are some specific things you can do to make things go as smoothly as possible.

1. Make sure that the icon they need to open is the first thing they see when they get to the computer. This cuts out many confusing steps and directions. They can get to work faster while still learning to open applications. If they have trouble opening the program, the class is off to a rough start.

2. Have stools or chairs ready so the kids are not killing time looking for something to sit on, dragging chairs around, or playing. If kids have a hard time sitting properly in a chair, make them stand!

3. With kindergartners and first graders, open a word processor and set the style and font for them before they get to the computer. It takes them a long time to write; why waste time on these details? The children can learn about fonts when they're a little older.

4. Create handouts with written directions and screen shots when necessary. Screen shots are pictures you can take of the computer screen, which you can copy and paste into a document. On a Macintosh, simultaneously press the shift+apple+3 keys to take a screen shot. A file called "picture" is added to the hard drive. Open the file and print. On a Windows machine, press the alt+printscreen keys to capture the active window. Open any drawing or word-processing program, and then paste the picture and print. Or you can press the printscreen key to print the entire screen. These handouts allow you to find out where students are and say (pointing), "You're at number four. Continue following the directions from here." With older students, you can explain the directions once to the entire class and then let individuals follow the written directions on their own at a lab or classroom computer station.
5. Pair kids to learn a new skill that's difficult or has many steps.
6. Have a backup plan. If everything fails, pull out a good book and read a story to your students.